MW01001034

THE HISTORY OF

ROME

IN 12 BUILDINGS

—— THE HISTORY OF ——

ROME

——— IN 12 BUILDINGS ———

A TRAVEL COMPANION
TO THE HIDDEN SECRETS
OF THE ETERNAL CITY

BY PHILLIP BARLAG

This edition first published in 2018 by New Page Books, an imprint of
Red Wheel/Weiser, LLC
With offices at:
65 Parker Street, Suite 7
Newburyport, MA 01950
www.redwheelweiser.com
www.newpagebooks.com

ISBN: 978-1-63265-132-7

Library of Congress Cataloging-in-Publication Data

CIP Data Available Upon Request.

Cover design by Joanna Williams
Large Piazza Navona photo by Emicristea/dreamstime
Colosseum photo by vaivirga/shutterstock
Scala Sancta photo by Aleksandr Stepanov/dreamstime
Ara Pacis museum photo by Giuseppemasci/dreamstime
Forum of Augustus photo by Iainhamer/dreamstime
Spine and back cover images courtesy of the author
Interior by PerfecType, Nashville, Tennesse
Typeset in Fairfield LT Std and Myriad Pro

Printed in Canada
MAR
10 9 8 7 6 5 4 3 2 1

For Erin. Where you are Gaia, I am Gaius.

CONTENTS

PREFACE

first went to Rome in early 2003. My wife and I had been married for just over a year, and had taken advantage of a deeply discounted airline fare. Our tickets were $330 for a round trip. A dollar more and we couldn't have afforded it; like so many newlyweds, we were broke.

When we landed at the airport, we took a train to Termini station. As the train approached the city, it slid through a gap in a massive ancient wall. I was awestruck. It was one thing to see the wall from either side, but by passing through it, we got a unique look at how massive this structure was. I wanted to know more. After asking around, I was told that these were the Walls of Aurelian.

Who was *Aurelian?*

I'd heard of Marcus Aurelius. Was that the same person? It occurred to me that I knew the Roman Empire had dominated what is now Europe for a long time. I had heard of Caesar, Nero, Caligula, and Constantine, but knew very little about them. The name "Caesar Augustus" rang a bell; was this the same as Caesar? There was a lot to learn.

I loved Rome; we had an amazing time. We walked countless miles every day, crisscrossing the city, taking in as much as we could. There was greater depth to the history of the city and its people than I could have imagined. My knowledge needed some augmentation. I vowed that if I ever returned, then I would be well-prepared.

That first trip sparked an interest in Roman history that I carry to this day. I have learned a lot about the city, the people, and the Empire. The more I learned, the more I found myself saying, "I wish I had known that when I was in Rome!"

This book is written to provide stories, ideas, and secrets that will make a trip to Rome more enjoyable, vivid, and satisfying. I have endeavored to write the book I wish I'd had for myself before my first trip to Rome. This book is not only for first-time visitors, but also to help anyone revisiting Rome have an even greater appreciation of what awaits.

I've been back to Rome several times. No matter how much I think I know, I always learn more, experiencing the city anew. Rome is known as the Eternal City; it's an appropriate moniker. Whether someone is going for their first time or their hundredth, there's always something awaiting discovery. All that's needed is knowing where to start.

INTRODUCTION

Every trip to Rome is special. No matter how many times someone has been there, nothing compares to the feeling you get when you arrive in the city and look around. It's magnificent . . . and overwhelming.

Think of Rome as a sprawling, outdoor museum. Within this museum there is a special exhibition: the sights of ancient Rome. Any good museum curates its collections to tell a distinct story. Nothing has a need for curation like a trip to Rome.

This book is a way to have a curated experience in Rome, with each chapter covering a different period of Rome's history, brought to life through the places and buildings of the city. There's something special about standing next to a monument and knowing the context— not just who built it, but why.

There are twelve chapters to this book. Each chapter is divided into three sections. The first is a close look at the history of a building or monument. The second is a guide to a few close-by dining options, as well as websites for travel information (hours, admission fees, and so on). The third takes a quick look at another building that continues the story before moving on.

This book will use the Colosseum as a point of common reference for walking and travel times. The Colosseum is in the middle of all of Rome's landmarks and, should anyone ever get lost, any local can help you find your way back there. All sections will give you walking times from the Colosseum, as well as the closest Metro station. A good, laminated street map would greatly aid your time in Rome (the Borch map is excellent, as is Michelin's). Some monuments have their own websites and phone numbers. Others point visitors to a centralized tourist information line. Dining options are rated on a one to three dollar sign scale.

This book is organized chronologically, not geographically. Some places are close to one another; others further afield. If you visit the buildings in the order they appear, then you will find yourself crisscrossing the city. This can be rewarding, giving the traveler the chance to make their own discoveries at points in between.

One way to use this book is to read each section before you visit the building. Another is to read all the chapters and then decide what you want to see for your-self. Yet a third is to pull it out when you arrive at any of the locations. For those who would like to dive deeper into the history of ancient Rome, there is a comprehen-sive bibliography to spur ideas for further reading.

Whether you are planning a trip to Rome, already there, or just interested in the city's history, I hope you enjoy this book and find it helpful.

Let's get started.

───── CHAPTER 1 ─────

Via Sacra

All roads lead to Rome—or so the saying goes. What is now a way of saying, "There are many ways to get to the same outcome," was once much closer to literal truth.

The idea of empire is so deeply associated with ancient Rome it is sometimes difficult to remember a time before empire, a time when Rome was just one ambitious and expansionist city on a continent of ambitious and expansionist cities.

Nothing tells the story of the rise of Rome, from its mythological founding at the teats of a wolf mother to its glorious empirical heights than its roads—and one road in particular, the Via Sacra, or Sacred Way, may tell the legend best.

Let us begin with those first Romans—the twins Romulus and Remus. After being abandoned in a basket by the Tiber River by their mother, they were suckled by a benevolent she-wolf. There they were found by a kindly shepherd and his wife, who raised them until becoming aware of their origins. It turns out that Mom was a priestess and the daughter of a deposed king of a nearby city. Once the twins figured out their regal connection, they helped their grandfather reclaim his throne, then set out to create a kingdom of their own.

Legend has it that Romulus wanted to found their settlement on the Palatine Hill, whereas Remus preferred the Aventine. The argument boiled over; Romulus murdered his brother and became the first king of Rome. The Palatine it was, then. From that day forward, an address on the Palatine Hill defined fashion, elegance, and power. Today, it is the origin of words such as "palace" and "palatial."

It is unlikely that Romulus and Remus were historical figures, but violence and bloodshed lie at the root of the Roman legend, an appropriate foreshadowing of the Roman legacy. From the time of its founding—often given as 753 BCE—Rome existed in a near-constant state of warfare. Romulus and his descendants fought war after war, securing Rome's place as a regional power in central Italy.

When soaking up the sights in the Forum,
don't forget to look down and contemplate the
history of the path beneath your feet.

As Rome's power spread, so too did the Forum, a complex of buildings and public spaces that came to be the center of life for Romans of all walks of life. Rich and poor, patrician and plebian, proud and humble, people from every slice of Roman society mingled there. Part outdoor market, part gathering place, the Forum is where court cases were decided, vendors hocked their wares, and business deals were struck. As Rome grew a greater foothold, the Forum grew with it.

Rome's second king, Numa Pompilius, was unusual for a Roman ruler in that he eschewed war for peace. He added the Temple of Janus to the Forum. The Roman god Janus was a deity of transitions. He looked after things such as birth, death, time, and doorways. Numa's temple doors would be opened in times of war and closed in times of peace. He promptly closed the doors, symbolizing that, through his rule, Rome was at peace.

Unfortunately, the doors of Numa's Temple of Janus were flung open by his successor, the war-loving Tullus Hostilius, who returned to expansionism and sent armies back into battle. The doors to the Temple of Janus would remain open for the next 400 years. That's a long time to be at war.

After four centuries of constant warfare, the Romans had dramatically expanded their sphere of influence.

Finally, an exhausted populace celebrated as the doors were closed, heralding a new era of peace and prosperity. And there they would stay—closed—signaling peace after 400 years of fighting . . . for all of eight years. It would be another two centuries of war—of the doors staying open. The Romans got in a lot of fights.

Although these legendary figures in early Roman history likely didn't exist, the Temple of Janus was real enough and the arc of history works. It is possible the historians invented the early kings of Rome to fit the known chronology. It's not clear how these myths arose, but it is clear that Rome was at war. A lot.

After 250 years of the capricious and unaccountable rule of kings, in 509 BCE the frustrated aristocrats of Rome overthrew the monarchy and instituted a Republic led by a Senate. This did nothing to abate their martial spirit. They fought on.

When visiting Rome, it's hard to remember its rise was not inevitable; the signs of empire and conquest are everywhere, but it took many centuries to forge the empire—year after year, decade after decade, century after century, and war after bloody war. The Roman armies marched off time and time again, extending the influence of the city further and further, bit by bit. Consider that it took nearly 650 years before the Romans comfortably controlled the Italian peninsula. Its rise wasn't spectacular. It was gradual and *relentless.*

As they conquered, they built roads. Roads made it faster, safer, and more efficient to move armies over the Italian peninsula and gave the Romans a huge military advantage. Rome's most famous road, the Appian Way, was built in 312 BCE to speed the army's route south to suppress their troublesome neighbors.

Each new wave of Roman expansion found another people and more cities reluctant to yield power and privileges to the bellicose city on the Tiber River. Yet, more often than not, the Romans won. Victory brought glory to Rome and to the victorious general. Usually, the Romans simply expected victory. On very rare occasions, they decided to celebrate. A Roman victory parade was called a Triumph. For a Roman general, a Triumph was the highest honor that they could receive.

This celebratory parade was the pinnacle of a career, and spilled over into a massive public festival across the city. For centuries, Roman generals fought abroad in the hopes of being awarded the right to celebrate a Triumph. On the big day, the winning general wore a gold-embroidered purple toga. His face was painted blood red in honor of the chief Roman god, Jupiter. For just a day, the general could look semi-divine and kingly. After the overthrow of the monarchy, the Romans detested even the hint of kingship; to have such aspirations could be a death sentence. The Romans were paradoxically in awe of individual power and repulsed by it, so in order to keep the conquering hero grounded, a slave would ride along in the general's chariot and whisper in his ear a warning: "Remember, thou art but a man." In other words, "Don't get any ideas. . . ."

Part of the Triumphal regalia was a laurel wreath. Depictions of this iconic wreath have come to be one of the most ubiquitous symbols of strength, accomplishment, and victory. Most people have seen the image of the laurel wreath countless times. In this crown lies the origins of the expression, "Don't rest on your laurels," cautioning generals not to over rely on their military conquest or the adulation of the people.

On the day of the Triumph, the general would line up his parade outside of the sacred boundary, or city line, called the pomerium. This was the only time soldiers were permitted to march inside the city lines, and the parade would duly wind itself across the boundary and into the city.

Throngs of people would pour out into the streets, waving laurel sprigs and anxiously waiting to cheer the glorious accomplishments of the mighty Romans. As the parade grew closer to the center of the city, the crowds grew larger and louder, reaching a fever pitch as the procession neared the Forum.

The general's chariot would be the focal point in a parade that included displays of the acts of heroism of the commander, spoils of war, and, when possible, captured and vanquished enemies marching in chains. For the hero, the greater the victory, the greater the show.

The culmination of the Triumph was entering the Forum by the Via Sacra, the Sacred Way. The final act was for the general to make his way through the adoring crowds and to the Temple of Jupiter. As the awed crowd watched, the general would ascend the steps and offer sacrifices to the chief god of the Roman pantheon.

After the sacrifices, the public would join in feasting, paid for by the largesse of the victorious general, eating and drinking themselves silly. Games and theatre performances were also staged in the city. The party could last for days.

Triumphs were exceedingly rare. Rome's conquests came in fits and starts, stretched through centuries. A citizen might go a lifetime without seeing one. When they happened, it was a big deal.

Of course, the Via Sacra wasn't only used for Triumphs. In many ways, it was also ancient Rome's main street. This path, which seems so humble today, was where Rome conducted its business, a route that Romans walked, every day, into and out of the Forum.

Untold millions of Romans, including the greatest among them, have walked the Via Sacra. With each footstep on the Via Sacra, you are walking with the titans of Roman history—Cicero, Pompey, Caesar, Augustus. You are watching as chariots clatter through the streets amid the adoring cheers of millions, celebrating another addition to the ever-lasting glory of Rome.

It's easy enough to overlook. Many of the paving stones have been lost through the millennia. Many that remain are irregularly shaped and dusty. It's not a wide or grand boulevard. In fact, in some places, it's just a few feet wide. Lost among the great buildings of Rome, this road doesn't get the attention it deserves.

When you are in the Forum on the Via Sacra, don't just look at the soaring monuments; look down at the deceptively humble road beneath your feet; remember that nothing was witness to the rise of Rome like it. With each step on the Via Sacra, you are walking in the footsteps of Rome's greatest historical figures, and untold millions of others. The story of Rome was written along the Via Sacra. Rome didn't just arrive at the top of the world order. It walked there.

➤ How to get to the Via Sacra

The Via Sacra is within the Imperial Forums (admission fee required). There are two ways to get into the Forum: one, a block south of the Colosseum, the other, a block west from the Colosseum along the Via Dei Fori Imperiali (the main thoroughfare running alongside the Imperial Forums). Whether you are walking from the Colosseum or coming from the Colosseo Metro station (Line B), it's a short walk of about ten minutes to either entrance.

Once inside the Forum, it's easy to find the Via Sacra. It is the main street that connects many of the landmarks, such as the Arch of Septimius Severus, the Temple of Antoninus and Faustina, and the Basilica of Maxentius.

➤ Local eats

Grab an inexpensive pizza or pasta dish in a down-to-earth spot:

Trattoria Pizzeria Luzzi ($)
Via di San Giovanni in Laterano 88, 00184
+39 06 709 6332
www.trattorialuzzi.it/

Trust the daily special to surprise and delight:

La Taverna dei Fori Imperiali ($$)

Via della Madonna Dei Monti 9, 00184

+39 06 679 8643

www.latavernadeiforiimperiali.com/

Debate what's better: the five-diamond service or the fantastic views of ancient sites:

Ristorante Aroma at Palazzo Manfredi ($$$)

Via Labicana 125, 00184

+39 06 7759 1380

www.aromarestaurant.it/en/

➤ Want more of the story before the next chapter? *Stop by the Forum Boarium.*

The Roman Forum gets all the love. It and its friends, the forums of Trajan, Augustus, and the like, get a lot of attention. They should. Their buildings and monuments tell great stories: Roman armies vanquishing foes and expanding the borders, heroes cementing their legacy in stone, gods shining their protection down from heaven. But they don't tell the *whole* story. In fact, there's another forum, just down the road, that has something important to say: the Forum Boarium.

Whereas its more famous cousins are named for the great people of Roman history, or for the city itself, the Forum Boarium is named for . . . cattle.

Rome's eventual mastery of the known world was by no means assured. At the time of its founding, it was just another settlement on just another hill. But Rome was well-situated and had geographic advantages that gave it a leg up. The hills were defensible. It overlooked a fordable bend in the river. Most importantly, it had access to the ocean via the Tiber, yet was still inland enough to be shielded from pirates and coastal raiders. As the city grew and projected its power outward, Rome needed a hub of commercial activity to support its growth. This is the Forum Boarium.

The most notable buildings are the two ancient temples, the Temple of Hercules (the round one) and the Temple of Portunus (the rectangular one). Hercules was, of course, the legendary hero of superhuman strength. His temple is the oldest surviving marble building in Rome. Portunus was the god of doors, gateways, locks, and livestock. This was an appropriate area for a temple to the god; the Romans needed him here. The Forum Boarium was the true commercial heart of Rome. It was where the docks were located. Grain and livestock poured into the city to feed the growing populace. Granaries were there to store food for emergencies. Goods from all over the world made their way to Rome through the docks. In many ways, it was the gateway to Rome.

This was the forum for the working man, the longshoremen of ancient Rome. This was the area where Rome was fed and clothed, where goods from luxuries to basic necessities worked their way into the economy. It seems appropriate the first gladiator games in Rome were fought there three centuries before the Colosseum opened.

While Roman armies marched over land, Roman merchants plied the waters of the Mediterranean. Opportunistic businessmen crossed Rome's frontiers, chasing the next deal, the next fortune. Often, it was merchants, not armies, who made first contact with foreigners. Roman soldiers stayed close to their barracks, while Roman traders brazenly went forward into the unknown. Rome's primary business was business, not war.

As you walk around, consider what it took to build the Roman Empire. More than armies, the workers and merchants of the Forum Boarium deserve their share of the credit too. Perhaps give a tip of the hat to Portunus. He might not be the most glamorous god in the Roman pantheon, but he did his job well.

The Temple of Hercules. The famous Mouth of Truth (Bocca della Verità) likely was a drain cover inside this temple.

The Temple of Portunus, dedicated to the god of locks, keys, and livestock. It and the Temple of Hercules are the oldest marble buildings in Rome.

Address: Piazza della Bocca della Verità.

Nearest Metro: Circo Massimo, Line B (twelve-minute walk), a twenty-minute walk from the Colosseum.

Tip: Be sure to look for the Mouth of Truth (Bocca della Verità), just inside the portico of Santa Maria in the Cosmedin. Legend has it that if you lie while your hand is in the mouth, then it will be cut off.

CHAPTER 2

Mamertine Prison

There are more than 900 churches in Rome. It can be hard to tell them apart. It's near impossible to see them all. Rome is, after all, the headquarters of one of the world's major religions, and centuries of emperors, foreign conquerors, popes, and kings have set out to display their benevolence and cement their legitimacy by building churches. When drawing up a list of things to do in Rome, the most famous churches—St. Peter's, San Giovanni in Laterano, Santa Maria Maggiore—are the usual. But one church, though humble compared to the majesty of its famous cousins, has an important story to tell, not about the Catholic Church, but about pagan Rome's quest for empire.

It's easy to overlook; the façade of San Giuseppe dei Falegnami is not particularly ornate. It doesn't matter

The northwest end of the Roman Forum. The Arch of Septimius Severeus is to the right; the building to the left is the church housing the Mamertine Prison. The empty space is the former site of the Temple of Concord.

anyway; the church is closed to the public. The reason to visit this humble church is not for what's inside, but for what lies beneath. The church is built atop a much older building, one with a dark history.

Find the church. Then find the side entrance into the museum. By stepping off the street, you are traveling back thousands of years. Descend into the Mamertine Prison. With each step down, you go further back in time, to the life and death struggle at the heart of the Roman world.

Ancient Rome was defined by strife and conflict. Romans fought among themselves for political power. Classes fought with one another to assert their rights. More than anything, Rome fought with any city or foreign nation that stood in the way of its relentless expansion. Romans were aggressive, with neighbor and foreigner alike.

As the little village on the Palatine grew, class conflict became more frequent. The families that traced their lineage back to the good old days with Romulus considered themselves to be of a higher order than everyone else. These families—the patricians—dominated political life in Rome for centuries. When the last king was tossed aside and the Republic was established, the patricians became even more insufferable. They controlled the government, the military, and the economy. They held the reins of power and liked it. Everyone else was not nearly as enamored of the situation.

The people outside the formal power structure, the plebeians, grew tired of this situation. By the time the 500s BCE came to a close, things had reached a boiling point. The plebeians were the hard-workers, whose labor was the backbone of the Roman economy. Tired of their oppression, and lack of representation in government, a huge swath of the population quit the city. In what might be the world's first labor strike, plebeians left Rome to camp out in protest on a hill outside of the city. Eventually, they struck a deal with the patricians for greater class equality and better access to elected office, but the harmony was tenuous. It would flare up from time to time, occasionally bringing the economy to a standstill.

Disagreements between the classes were stunting Rome's growth. Not long after the first strike, the ambiguity of the legal system had to be addressed. In 449 BCE, after careful work and several drafts by appointed committees, Roman elders published a thorough, formal law code. Called the Twelve Tables, the Roman society now had explicit rules to govern things such as the conduct of its citizens, and the class distinction between patrician and plebeian. More than 300 years since its founding, Rome was on firm footing when it came to law and order. The Twelve Tables were one of the most sophisticated law codes of the ancient world; they are still influencing law around the world today.

As the Roman system matured into a society bound by law and courts, defenses and prosecutions, it oddly lacked something that we closely associate with such modern institutions: prisons.

For a society so enamored with the law, and saturated with the rhetoric of right and wrong, it seems surprising that the concept of imprisonment was foreign to the Romans. If someone had broken a law or a social contract, or proven to be an implacable enemy of the Republic, then they needed to be gotten rid of, not held in perpetual confinement at the expense of the state. You were either guilty or innocent, a free citizen or an enemy. You could either live in Rome freely, or be exiled or executed. It makes sense for the Romans, who had a god dedicated to boundaries, to draw such clear lines.

That didn't mean legal cases were always quickly adjudicated, or that authorities always knew what to do with people right away. In some cases, it was useful to hang on to an enemy of the state for a while to maximize their utility for political propaganda. Even the Romans needed a place to store prisoners, even if temporarily, until they could be dealt with.

Being a Roman citizen granted people a right to a trial with a jury of peers. (Sound familiar? It's the Twelve Tables!) Some trials were legitimate, conducted by fair and impartial juries. Others were shams, where political expediency outweighed fairness, and judgments were predetermined and rushed through. Either way, people occasionally found themselves locked up as their cases progressed through the court system.

The most notable detainees were not Roman citizens awaiting trial, but foreign enemies awaiting humiliation. As Rome's legions went further and further afield, conquering strange and exotic peoples, generals sought to outdo one another with their victory celebrations. The culmination of any victory—a Senate-awarded Triumph for the victorious general—was a very big deal. The greater the party, the greater was the glory for the conquering hero.

The true show-stopper was to capture your enemies alive, and march them in chains for all the people to see. It must have been humiliating; being taken captive while fighting to defend your homeland from foreign invaders, carted off in chains to a far-away capital full of strange people speaking an indecipherable language, only to

*The stone and marble altar to Saints Peter and
Paul (Paul is on the right, Peter the left).*

be marched in front of a chariot driven by your smug enemy, while hundreds of thousands of people jeered and mocked you. After the Triumph, the foreign captors were no longer of any use. Nor were those convicted of treason or capital offense.

The fate that awaited most people in the Mamertine Prison was not prison, but rather banishment or death. It was from here that convicts were sent off to execution. After suffering the jeering of Roman crowds, foreign captives were taken back and strangled, their usefulness to the Romans being exhausted by their public shaming. As Roman influence spread to dominate the Mediterranean—and beyond—it was through this obscure place that countless people came to await their fate. Each coup foiled, every foreign leader captured, every political enemy quietly disposed: To descend the steps into the Mamertine Prison is to walk, step by step, with Rome as it ruthlessly feasted on those who stood in her way.

Through its centuries of use, some of Rome's most deadly foreign enemies and dangerous political dissidents were contained within its walls, to await their fate. Many entered, but fewer left.

In Roman society, if the state deemed your life to be forfeit, then your property was too; the state took possession and was enriched, nourished by the blood of its victims. Too often in Roman history, political opponents became victims of the state not because of anything they said or did, but because someone coveted their assets. If its walls could talk, then the Mamertine would share terrible stories that underwrite the complicated legacy of Rome's Empire. But walls can't talk; and the voices of the extinguished fall mute.

Well, not all of them. Lest we get too macabre, not all of the victims of this terrible and complicated place are lost to history. It is believed that this is the place that Saints Peter and Paul were held before their executions in the Christian persecution following the Great Fire of Rome in 64 CE. As a Roman citizen, Paul was afforded the dignity of beheading. As a noncitizen, Peter was crucified. Both left from the Mamertine to meet their fates. Today, there is a stone altar to commemorate the martyrs. Hints of medieval frescoes commemorated the exalted founders of the Christian church. To be in the Mamertine Prison is not just to be among the dead; it is to be among the remembered, to be present at the early days of a family of religions that would grow to eventually count one in three people on the planet as a follower.

The Mamertine Prison is fascinating . . . and eerie. It's unsettling being in a place that has witnessed suffering and bloodshed, to stand in the very place where others have died. Descend to the lowest level and look up through a grated drain cover. Imagine a prisoner being lowered by rope into the ancient cistern. Feel the claustrophobia of the tight walls, and then consider a dozen or more other prisoners sharing the space. Breathe the dank air; close your eyes to take away the modern lighting. It's hard not to shiver thinking about what it was like to be a prisoner there.

But as much as a physical, tangible experience, the Mamertine Prison elicits a series of ideas, concepts, and memories of people that have come and gone, each important in telling the story of ancient Rome. To be there is to gain insight into the foundation of Roman law, and to remember that justice means something very different now than it did 2,000 years ago. It also speaks to a contradiction at the heart of the Roman story: For all the Romans' lofty rhetoric about liberty and freedom, they could have a callous indifference to the value of life.

➤ How to get to the Mamertine Prison

Access is through a side entrance underneath the church San Giuseppe dei Falegnami (Saint Joseph the Carpenter). The church is not currently open to the public. Admission is required to go the Mamertine Prison. It is directly across from the Arch of Septimius Severus, a very hard-to-miss landmark. The walk to the building is approximately twelve minutes, whether by the Colosseo Metro station (Line B) or from the Colosseum.

Address: Clivo Argentario, 1.

Phone number: +39 06 698961

➤ Hours

Monday to Sunday from 8:30 a.m. to 6:15 p.m.
Official website: *http://tullianum.org/?lang=en.*

➤ Local eats

Indulge in good gelato, even if you're dairy-free:
Gelateria La Dolce Vita ($)
Via Cavour 306, 00184
+39 06 8892 2877

Continue roaming after loading up on delicious, carry-out pasta:
Pasta Chef, Street Food Gourmet ($$)
Via Baccina 42, 00184
+39 06 488 3198
www.pastachefroma.it/it/home/

Taste the best of Ireland in Rome:
>   The Surge Irish Pub ($$)
>   Via Della Madonna Dei Monti 110, 00184
>   *www.facebook.com/thesurgepubroma*

➤ Want more of the story before the next chapter? *Stop by the Temple of Concord.*

There is something oddly satisfying about looking at a totally ruined building, when so little is left of the original that it's hard for even the most imaginative onlooker to complete the picture in the mind's eye. Satisfying, that is, if you know the secret of what once occupied the space and the meaning of the emptiness. As people walk the Forum, they may not take note of the site once occupied by the Temple of Concord, but they should.

The Romans had a god or goddess for everything. True to form, the Romans crowned the goddess Concordia, and tasked her to make sure that everyone was getting along. Concordia's job was to ensure harmony.

The Romans' religious piety bordered on paranoia. They believed that if their gods didn't get enough attention, they would grow restive, then angry and vengeful. To neglect a god or goddess for too long was an invitation to disaster. It was the duty of every Roman to remain pious, offering prayers and sacrifices to make sure the gods showered favor on Rome.

When facing a crisis, Romans would seek to proactively enlist a god or goddess on their side by vowing that if they emerged victorious, then they would build that god a nice, new temple. The idea was that the god would want the new home, and work from the heavens to arrange the desired outcome. When the people of Rome began to turn against each other, Concordia made a good choice. Though, it must be said that a pile of Roman corpses seemed an odd thing to trigger an homage to the goddess of harmony.

Crisis loomed over Rome in the last half of the second century BCE. It reached its apex in 122 BCE when the reformer Gaius Gracchus was hunted down and murdered at the hands of a vicious gang of Senators and paid assassins. The mob also butchered 3,000 of Gracchus's supporters. The organizer of this spasm of violence was none other than the sitting Consul, the highest elected officer in Rome. In his mind, by crushing the reform movement, peace could return. To mark the great deliverance of the city, he fulfilled a vow to Concordia to build her a temple. Despite the new home, Concordia wasn't bought off so easily. The crisis wasn't over; it had just been delayed.

In time, other reformers would rise and fall; each time their crusades would trigger a crisis that threatened the stability of the Roman system. Into this maelstrom, one of the titans of world history would step forward. Just a few decades after the death of Gracchus and the rebuilding of the Temple of Concordia, the rise of Julius Caesar was at hand.

Find the empty space where the Temple of Concord once stood, tucked neatly behind the Arch of Septimius Severus. There is a sign to mark the spot. The empty space is an apt metaphor for the decline and fall of the Roman Republic, and the near constant state of civil strife, war, and rivalry that defined Rome until the collapse of the Empire. The Romans apparently had other things to worry about than concord, but Concordia, it would seem, gave up on the Romans too. As they turned on one another, she turned away from them. We should not confuse emptiness for silence.

Address: Roman Forum.

Nearest Metro: Colosseo, Line B, a twelve-minute walk from both the station and the Colosseum.

CHAPTER 3

The Temple of Caesar

In many ways, the story of Rome *is* the story of Julius Caesar. His life and career spanned countless elements of Roman society, and served as the fulcrum in the transition from Republic to Empire. The Empire would not have been possible without him. Yet, for someone who left such a massive imprint on the Roman world, little of his legacy shows up in the city's buildings and monuments. The building that best tells the story of Caesar was not built in his lifetime. Rather, it starts with his death: the most famous assassination in history.

Caesar was born in 100 BCE. Just the year before, his uncle Marius had achieved a series of stunning military victories, defeating invading barbarians and cementing the security of the Italian peninsula. By the time of Caesar's birth, Marius held the consulship an astonishing six times and rode a wave of popularity with the people that no Roman had ever known. Marius was Caesar's uncle through marriage, the great general having married Caesar's aunt. It had been a political boon to Marius. He came from a middle-class family, without rank or prestige. Roman society was class obsessed. Caesar's family was in the upper echelons of the nobility. The marriage legitimized Marius by bringing him closer to the top of the social order. His family should have been an asset to young Caesar, but he had two things working against him.

The first is that although his family was distinguished, it was broke; its glory was in the past. Though high in the nobility, Caesar grew up in the slums. As a result, he identified much more with the common man than he did members of his own class. This connection was mutual, and in time, the bonds between Caesar and the people would be the hallmark of his life, and more dramatically, his death.

The second, and more ominous, was that not everyone loved Marius. He had a great rival, a former subordinate anxious for his turn at the top. Unlike Marius, Sulla was of noble rank. Marius's populism rankled and the rivalry between the two would set off a series of civil wars that would culminate with the collapse of

The last resting spot of Julius Caesar.

the Republic. At one point in the back and forth, Sulla seized power and determined to liquidate his political enemies. He posted a list of people that were to be eliminated; their murders legally sanctioned, their property forfeit. Their children and grandchildren had their rights revoked. Under Sulla's reign of terror, enemies were butchered, and often their heads were displayed on pikes in the Forum. Sulla was a vindictive guy. Given Caesar's connections to Marius, his life fell into danger.

Thus, began a life of extraordinary adventure. Caesar's early years are better than fiction. Fleeing Sulla's death squads, he went on the run, hiding in basements, moving around only at night, and even being captured and bribing his way to freedom. He won individual glory in early military service. He survived capture and ransom by pirates and, when freed, attacked the same pirates, took back his ransom money, and crucified them all. He took on corrupt governors, fighting for the poor and dispossessed against the members of his own class. With every step in his career, Caesar forged deeper and deeper connections to the everyday citizens of Rome. No matter what his family pedigree, he was their champion, and they were his political base.

His populism was more than opportunism; the people loved Caesar. He loved them back. What the love and affection of the people couldn't buy, cold hard cash could. Caesar borrowed heavily to finance his career, and he chalked up win after win at the ballot box. The highest office was the consulship; two were elected each year to prevent any individual from having too much power. Caesar won the consulship in his first year of eligibility. He'd come a long way, but was still young and lacked the political capital needed to execute his ambitious reform package, centered on assistance to the poor and landless. Accordingly, he organized the famous First Triumvirate with the two men at the top of the pecking order: Crassus and Pompey.

At first, their alliance went well; all three were able to gain from their association with each other. Pompey married Caesar's beloved daughter, Julia, making the older Pompey son-in-law to the younger Caesar. After a few years, things began to unwind. Crassus was eager to win glory on the battlefield, and picked a fight with Rome's dreaded enemy, the Parthians. He got himself killed in the process. After his death, the Parthians are said to have poured molten gold down his throat to slake his insatiable thirst for money. When Crassus died, Caesar and Pompey drifted from collaboration to rivalry.

Julia died in childbirth, and the last bonds between the two were severed. Factions lined up behind them.

Get up close and personal with Caesar at the
spot of his impromptu funeral pyre.

Pompey aligned himself with the Senate, assuming the mantle of defender of conservative institutions. Caesar was the champion of the people. Caesar sought to repair the relationship, offering his great niece Octavia as bride. Pompey rebuffed the offer and all efforts at conciliation. War loomed.

By this point, 49 BCE, Caesar had been military governor abroad for nearly a decade. The stalemate between Pompey and the Senate on one side, and Caesar on the other, escalated into civil war when Caesar crossed the Rubicon river, the official border separating Rome from its provinces. Spooked by Caesar's aggressiveness, Pompey fled Rome, leaving the city undefended. Caesar entered the city, promised the people that there would be no Sulla-style proscription, and took off after his former son-in-law. Pompey fled to Greece; Caesar followed. After a series of battles, Caesar emerged victorious and Pompey fled again, this time to Egypt. As he approached the shore, agents of the king, Ptolemy XIII, had Pompey beheaded.

Caesar continued to campaign all over Africa and Europe, mopping up resistance and accumulating more power. Eventually, he made his way back to Rome, assuming dictatorial powers. Unlike his predecessors, he never indulged in bloody purges. On the contrary, Caesar's policy had always been to offer pardon to enemies, finding grace in victory a more stable long-term policy than liquidation of the vanquished. Slowly, peace returned. The exhausted people were grateful. Families had been torn apart in the constant conflict. Despite his patrician rank, Caesar never forgot his humble origins in the slums. No matter how high he rose, he always cultivated a loving relationship with the rank and file citizens.

His fellow oligarchs seethed. Not only was Caesar hording all the powers of state, normally distributed across many different elected offices, but he was also circumventing the traditional social norms, which elevated the rich at the expense of the poor. They plotted their revenge.

Caesar awoke on the famous day, the Ides of March, 44 BCE, not feeling well. His wife had a bad dream, in which he had been murdered. She begged him to stay home. He sent word to the Senate that he was ill and would not be in attendance at the day's meeting. He was scheduled to embark on a military campaign the next day. The Senators panicked; this was to be the day they struck Caesar down. Miss this day and Caesar would march off on campaign, and cloak himself in more martial glory. This was their last chance.

Desperate, they sent someone Caesar would trust: Decimus Brutus, a distant cousin of Caesar, as well as the famous Marcus Brutus, one of Caesar's trusted lieutenants. Caesar's patronage had brought Decimus military appointments and political offices alike. Caesar loved Decimus like a son, and said so in public on many occasions. When Decimus arrived to talk Caesar into attendance at the Senate meeting, Caesar listened. Off they went, arm in arm.

Fire had damaged the Senate house, and the meeting was to be held in the Theatre of Pompey, an opulent building and the first stone theatre built in Rome. Caesar's rival had built the enormous theatre with booty from his overseas conquests. Conspiracies were hard to keep secret, and an ally of Caesar had gotten wind of the plot. He frantically sent a messenger off to meet Caesar to issue the warning. The messenger arrived and fought his way through the crowd, handing Caesar the message and exhorting him to read it. In the crush of Senators making their way into the meeting, he wasn't able to step aside to read the dispatch.

Once the meeting began, the Senators wasted little time. Caesar sat in a chair and a Senator came forward to present a petition. In short order, dozens of Senators pulled daggers from under their togas, hacking and stabbing wildly, striking down the man of the people, and often stabbing each others in the frantic burst of violence. After the deed was done, conspirators and unknowing witnesses alike fled the theatre. Alone and unconscious on the cold marble floor, Caesar bled to death under the unblinking stare of a statue of Pompey the Great. He never read the warning. Several hours later, a few servants slipped back into the empty theatre to collect Caesar's body.

The conspirators thought they had restored the Republic and liberated the people from a tyrant. They thought they were heroes. They thought they could sell their vision to the people. They thought wrong.

Furious at having their champion taken away, the people rioted. The conspirators barricaded themselves inside their homes or fled. The unrest was only beginning.

The city was on edge on the day of Caesar's funeral. As befitting a high-profile noble, Caesar's funeral took place in the Forum. A huge crowd came out to pay homage. The restive crowd grew increasingly angry as the reality of Caesar's death sank in. Caesar's lieutenant, Marc Antony, sensed an opportunity.

Antony stood before the crowd and whipped them up into a frenzy, reminding the people of all the things Caesar had done for them, and heaping accusations and insults on the conspirators. With the crowd in a fever pitch, Antony held up the toga that Caesar was wearing on the Ides, pointing to the stab wounds, to all his blood.

Angry shouts erupted from the crowd, which grew bigger and bigger with each passing minute.

Then came the last straw. Antony read out Caesar's will to the seething crowd. It contained many shockers, but the people heard one thing above all. In death, Caesar donated his estates, gardens, sizable art collection, and a considerable amount of his cash to the people of Rome for their enrichment. Far from being the oppressor of the people, in death Caesar proved whom he loved above all: the people of Rome. *This* was the monster from whom they had been liberated?! In the eyes of the citizens, the assassination wasn't liberation, it was theft; their champion had been stolen from them.

Rioting erupted; angry Romans began tearing the Forum apart. They grabbed benches from the courts, branches from the trees, throwing anything combustible on Caesar's pyre. The funeral turned into a conflagration; flames swept through the Forum. Bent on revenge, the mob crashed through the streets and made for the homes of Marcus Brutus and Cassius, the chief culprits of Caesar's murder. They only narrowly escaped, fleeing to Greece to prepare for the inevitable civil war. The conspirators' plans backfired. Rather than restore the Republic, they hastened its demise. In the ashes of the Republic would emerge the Empire, and in the place of Caesar would rise a man who would accumulate and consolidate greater powers and honors than anyone before, so singular a figure that history records him as the first Emperor of Rome.

When you visit the Forum, you will find the Temple of Caesar. Caesar's primary heir, Octavian, built the temple to honor the memory of the great man, and to remind people of his own connection to Caesar's legacy. Not much of the temple remains; like many things in the Forum, you need to use a lot of imagination to see what the building would have been in its full glory. But the most important part is still there, and it's a can't miss. Covered by a modern canopy, which helps mark the spot for visitors, is the very site of Caesar's pyre. Duck behind a stone wall, and you can stand alone with Caesar at his last resting spot. The centuries—and the distance between you and Caesar—vanish. Here is the place where the Romans poured out their grief and anguish. Here is the place that fire spilled out to burn down the Forum, and with it, the Republic. In this quiet spot, sheltered from the searing Roman sun, you can pay your respects, or reflect on the fleeting nature of fame and fortune. Above all, you can enjoy the company of the most transformational figure in Roman history—and perhaps of all time.

➤ How to get to the Temple of Caesar

The Temple of Caesar is in the middle of the Roman Forum along the Via Sacra. Look for the modern metal roof covering the site of Caesar's pyre. Whether you are walking from the Colosseum or coming from the Colosseo Metro station (Line B), it's a short walk of about ten minutes.

➤ Local eats

Grab hold of a hand-held pizza with great topping options:
    Trieste Pizza ($)
    Via Urbana 112, 00184
    +39 06 481 5319
    www.facebook.com/triestepizza.roma/

Choose from more than 100 wine options in a wine and tapas bar open since 1895:
    Ai Tre Scalini ($$)
    Via Panisperna 251, 00184
    +39 06 4890 7495
    www.aitrescalini.org

Splurge on high-end seafood:
    Matermatuta ($$$)
    Via Milano 48, 00184

+39 06 482 3962
www.matermatuta.eu/

➤ Want more of the story before the next chapter? *Stop by the Pyramid of Cestius.*

It's easy to be distracted these days, to lose track of where you are or where you're going. Should this happen to you in a little corner of Rome, you might look up and see a pyramid rising nearly one hundred feet high, and think for just a moment that you're in Egypt.

The Pyramid of Cestius is interesting to look at, but it represents more than an oddly out-of-place building. It's a symbol of what Rome was: the cultural hub of the known world.

When the pyramid was built in 12 BCE, Rome had been in domination of once mighty Egypt for decades. As the two great powers had come in contact with one another, a cultural exchange took place. Roman armies invaded Egypt. Egyptian culture invaded Rome.

Egypt was ancient, even to the Romans; we are closer in history to Cleopatra than she was to the construction of the Great Pyramids.

At the time of the Roman conquest, Egypt was fantastically wealthy. To the Romans, Egypt was exotic and

The Pyramid of Cestius.

luxurious. Like modern people keeping an eye on the latest from Milan, Egypt was downright fashionable. As the cultural exchange deepened, Rome was gripped by Egypt fever. Prominent Romans outdid one another to bring Egyptian artifacts back to Rome. People adopted Egyptian fashion. The cult of the Egyptian goddess Isis took hold; temples sprang up across the city. Obelisks were carted off and brought to the capital.

Rome was a cultural crossroads. One of the unintended effects of its expansion was that Rome brought people in contact that had no prior knowledge of one another. Much of what we know about many people of the ancient world comes not from their own histories, but from Roman accounts of contact. The Germanic tribes, for example, had no written languages, no bored and wealthy elites who picked up a pen to focus their efforts on history. Rome's expansionism filled in blanks on the map and gave modern historians priceless information about people of the ancient world.

We tend to think of the people that inhabited ancient Rome as Roman. But the reach of the Empire brought about cultural and ethnic diversity unmatched anywhere in the ancient world. As people were assimilated into the Roman way of life, it was only natural that some would make their way to Rome itself. The streets and markets buzzed with people of different cultures, religions, and regions. In many senses, ancient Rome was the first true melting pot.

That's why Cestius, a mid-level bureaucrat with too much cash, chose to emulate an ancient empire more than 1,000 miles away. He was showing off his sense of style, building his massive tomb in a trend that had gripped the city.

The pyramid today is only open on select days; reservations must be made in advance. The timing is tricky, but if just to walk around, to look up, and to admire, then it's worth the trip. Rome is more than the Romans. Even more than 2,000 years ago, it was the center of the cultural world. People came to the city from all over to shop, sightsee, visit, trade, and worship. Have things really changed all that much?

Address: Via Raffaele Persichetti.

Nearest Metro: Piramide, Metro Line B (three-minute walk), a twenty-four-minute walk from the Colosseum.

Tip: The Pyramid is open only for guided tours, and generally only on the first weekend of each month. Reservations must be made in advance by calling +39 06 5743193. Visit the following website for up-to-date information: *www.turismoroma.it/cosa-fare/piramide-cestia?lang=en.*

CHAPTER 4

Ara Pacis

Anyone interested in the sights and monuments of ancient Rome might be forgiven for looking past modern construction. It's easy to overlook steel and glass when you're looking for brick and marble. But in one case, a modern museum was built to encase a monument of great antiquity. Perhaps that's why this amazing structure is often overlooked. The Ara Pacis was an outdoor altar dedicated to peace, and the accomplishments of the Emperor Augustus. It is one of the most interesting pieces of imperialist propaganda ever.

Augustus is one of the towering figures of human history. The first and greatest Roman Emperor, he came to power through an unlikely path. He wasn't always called Augustus. In fact, Augustus wasn't a birth name; it was as an honorific meaning "revered one," bestowed later in life and well into his spectacular career. It would take him a long time to be so recognized.

He was born as Gaius Octavius into a reasonably prosperous family, but one step below the Senatorial order. His father was ambitious, and resolved to improve his family's fortunes. He had some success, but died young, when his son was just four. Ambition wasn't the only thing the father bequeathed to his son; he had married Atia, who happened to be the daughter of Julius Caesar's sister (meaning that the little boy was Caesar's great nephew).

Caesar had a shortage of male relatives to mentor. He began to notice his great nephew as Octavius entered his teenage years. This itself was unusual, as Octavius was a maternal relative, which carried little weight in paternalistic Roman society. Caesar's patronage was complicated for the young boy. Atia was an overbearing and overprotective mother. These two forces, his mother's desire to keep Octavius out of public life, and Caesar's need to have close family in his inner circle, came up against each other in dramatic fashion in 44 BCE. On the Ides of March, March 15th, Caesar was famously assassinated by a group of Senators jealous of his consolidation of power.

*The sculptural program that runs along the top of
the exterior of the altar. Note Agrippa with his head
covered at the center of the photo. By the time the altar
was completed and dedicated, Agrippa was dead.*

Caesar had died wealthy, with a substantial estate. However, he didn't have a son to whom he could pass his inheritance. He did have an illegitimate son with Cleopatra, whom history knows as Caesarion. But this boy couldn't be a Roman citizen, and therefore, not an heir. In death, Caesar solved a problem that he couldn't solve in life.

To the shock of everyone, including the young man himself, Caesar posthumously adopted his teenage great-nephew as his own son. At the time, Octavius was east, taking lessons in military strategy and oratory in preparation for public life. His mother begged him to deny the bequest and stay safe. His personal ambition outweighed his mother's pleading. He traveled to Rome and claimed his inheritance. By law, he was Caesar's son. As was his right, Octavius began calling himself by his adoptive name, Gaius Julius Caesar Octavianus. Nope, not confusing at all.

Atia was right to be worried. By accepting the legacy of the fallen Dictator, Octavius had put himself into the center of a maelstrom of violence, treachery, civil war, and bloodshed that lasted decades. That such things happened was no great surprise; Rome had been in a constant state of warfare—either with foreign enemies or between political factions—nearly from its founding.

What's surprising is that he emerged triumphant, and at the highest levels of power any Roman had ever achieved.

When the dust settled, the cowed and exhausted Senate bestowed upon Octavius the honorific "Augustus," or "revered one." He would maintain the charade of deferring to the Senate for key decisions, and they would maintain the charade that they believed it.

Once he was firmly in control, he set his sights on the same challenge that created his opportunity in the first place: succession planning. Like Caesar, Augustus had no male heirs, not even an illegitimate one. By the time his rise to power was reaching its apex, he was on his third marriage, to Livia, and still had no natural son.

He'd met Livia in 39 BCE when she was married, had a young son named Tiberius, and was six months pregnant with her second child. His own wife, Scribonia, was pregnant too, but he was smitten. In a confusing sequence of events, he divorced Scribonia on the very day that she gave birth to their daughter Julia, freeing him up to marry Livia. The only complications to be ironed out were her current marriage and her late-stage pregnancy. No problem. The husband, Tiberius Claudius Nero (yup, the family name Nero would show up a few decades later when *that* Nero became Emperor), was conveniently pushed aside, compelled to divorce Livia to

The altar.

make room for Octavius, or Caesar, or whatever he was called by then. Livia delivered her baby, a boy named Drussus, on January 14th. The happy couple was wed on January 17th. Nero gave the bride away to the man who had shoved him out of the marital bed. The Romans could be weird sometimes.

More than a decade into his marriage to Livia and still there was no male heir. Having a son just didn't seem to be in the cards, so Augustus made other arrangements. His first solution was to marry off his fourteen-year-old daughter, Julia, and focus on grandchildren. The lucky groom was none other than her own first cousin, Augustus's nephew Marcellus. All in the family . . . .

Marcellus was popular with the people, but he was young and lacked experience. Augustus sought his development, but the mentorship was cut short when Marcellus fell ill and died at about nineteen years old. The death of Marcellus seemed too convenient for many—both contemporaries and historians. A considerable number of people have cast a suspicious eye at Livia, the archetype of the evil step-mom, suspected of poisoning young Marcellus to keep the path clear for her own sons.

A sad widow produces no heirs, and at the ripe old age of eighteen, Julia was married again, this time to the right-hand man of dear old dad. Marcus Agrippa was a close friend of Augustus dating to their childhoods. Agrippa had been by Augustus's side from before he was Augustus, before he was Caesar, back when he was simply a provincial nobody. Agrippa had many virtues, but chief among them were his astonishing military, political, and logistical talent. As important, Agrippa was dutiful and devoted. From the earliest days of their partnership, Agrippa had always deferred to Augustus, truly content to be the "man behind the scenes." With a track record of unbroken loyalty going back decades, Augustus trusted Agrippa implicitly.

Agrippa was an energetic general and administrator. He was the architect of many of Augustus's military victories and the architect of countless buildings raised in the Emperor's name (he also put up a few in his own). He was thoroughly competent, and quite possibly the greatest right-hand man in history. He was also married, but by now it's pretty clear that this was no matter. He divorced his wife and married Julia—some twenty-five years his junior. Marriages in the nobility were about politics; they weren't supposed to be happy. But this one was and the couple seemed to have had genuine affection. They sure produced kids, including sons that played into Augustus's dynastic ambitions.

The first son by the marriage, Gaius, was born in 20 BCE. He was joined by little brother Lucius in 17 BCE. There was a sister in between, and eventually another sister and a final brother. Augustus now had grandsons on which to peg his dynastic hopes. He would see to their education and mentorship personally, and in 17 BCE, with little Lucius not a year old, Augustus adopted the two boys, making his grandsons his sons, bringing them into his house to oversee their education personally. Agrippa, as always, supported his patron's actions and watched as his kids left his house to be the children of another man.

By now it's understandable if these bizarre relationships are confusing. The imperial dynasty—known as the Julio-Claudian dynasty—is difficult to follow. The Roman people could be forgiven if they had a hard time following all of the back and forth, births, deaths, divorces, and remarriages.

Rome suffered through nearly two decades of civil war, first with Caesar, then Octavius/Augustus. Add to that centuries of near constant warfare with external foes; the Romans were a bellicose people. Augustus wanted to show the people that he had brought peace and stability. He had ended the civil wars, vanquished foreign enemies, and set up a stable family, ensuring prosperity for the Roman Empire for centuries to come.

He ordered the doors of the Temple of Janus closed for the first time in two centuries, but he wanted to make and even bolder statement.

That's what the Ara Pacis was for, an altar dedicated to the Augustan vision. It's adorned with imagery from Rome's history, of Augustus's accomplishments, and, most importantly, the Imperial Family. They're all there: Augustus, Livia, Gaius and Lucius, Agrippa and Julia, even the sulky Tiberius. The message to the Roman people was loud and clear. Peace had returned; the family was stable. Augustus was in control. The Ara Pacis was used for religious ceremony under the watchful eye of the cult of the Imperial Family. Their pious images looked down on the Roman people, signaling the ever-lasting glory of the regime.

When you walk into the museum that houses the Ara Pacis, you'll see these wonderful carvings, in relief across the top of the altar. The building is light and airy, complemented by displays and artifacts that add context to the times. It's a can't miss.

But for all the messages conveyed in its sculptural program, it contains a sad postscript. In between when construction began and when it was completed, Agrippa died at the age of fifty-one. After his death, Julia delivered their fifth and last child, appropriately named

Agrippa Posthumous. By the time the altar was consecrated, the great lieutenant to Augustus had been dead
for three years. Yet Agrippa is still there, piously clothed
as a priest and looking down with stoic benevolence.

All five of his children would suffer sad fates. Of
note, Gaius and Lucius would die young, breaking
Augustus's heart, shattering his dynastic plans, and cast-
ing countless more suspicious stares at Livia. Her ambitions would be realized when, out of options, Augustus
gave in and adopted Tiberius. Upon Augustus's death,
Tiberius assumed the unique role that Augustus had created. For sure, there are plenty of people who think that
wicked Livia poisoned her aged husband to make room
for her son.

In many ways, the Ara Pacis represents the height
of Augustan ambition and propaganda. By the time the
first sacrifices were made at the high altar, the message
carved in marble was already out of date, and the plans
of Rome's first emperor were unwinding. Agrippa was
dead. Gaius and Lucius would follow not long after. And
yet, Augustus ruled on.

You can walk with him, climbing the same steps
today that he did nearly 2,000 years ago. Ascend the
gentle stairs and climb inside. Imagine the sacrifices and
offerings, the pleas and vows Augustus offered to honor

the gods, to remember the deceased, and to remind the Roman people of his glory. His plans for succession may have been dashed time and time again, but the ultimate goal of securing an enduring and perpetual legacy was achieved.

The museum that houses the Ara Pacis is a striking contrast in its modernity, stitching together the world of two millennia ago and the world of today in one remarkable place. When you visit, you are hand-in-hand with Augustus, but you have the benefit of hindsight. You know which prayers of his were answered, and which were ignored.

➤ How to get to the Ara Pacis

The Ara Pacis is housed inside a modern structure, with other exhibits, artifacts, and sculpture. It is on the Tiber, in between the Ponte Margherita and the Ponte Cavour. It is a thirty-five-minute walk from the Colosseum and a twelve-minute walk from the Spagna Metro station (Line A). Admission is required.

Address: Lungotevere in Augusta, 00186.

Phone Number: +39 060608

Website: *http://en.arapacis.it/*

➤ Hours

Daily from 9:30 a.m. to 7:30 p.m.
   December 24 and 31, 9:30 a.m. to 2:00 p.m.
   Closed January 1, May 1, December 25

➤ Local eats

Grab a delicious sandwich on homemade bread:
   PataPinsa ($)
   Via del Vantaggio 42 piazza del popolo, via Flaminia
502 ponte milvio, 00186
   +39 06 3265 0256

Celebrate a special occasion in a romantic setting:
   Ad Hoc ($$$)
   Via Ripetta 43, 00186
   +39 06 323 3040
   www.ristoranteadhoc.com/en/default.html

Go upscale with great Italian dishes and a menu that has
English translations:
   L'Arcangelo ($$$)
   Via Giuseppe Gioacchino Belli 59, 00193
   +39 06 3210992
   www.larcangelo.com/contatti/

➤ Want more of the story before the next chapter? *Stop by the Forum of Augustus.*

Today, most of the Forum built by Rome's first Emperor is ruined. You will have to look hard to find the secret it holds. As you slowly take in the ruins, you'll notice that the whole complex seems slightly off balance. Should you come across a plan of the Forum, it will confirm your suspicions: The Forum of Augustus is asymmetrical. The Romans were engineering masters, capable of achieving architectural balance and symmetry. Augustus himself had unlimited financial means and political power. How could such an important complex be built with anything less than perfection? The answer helps solve one of the most interesting paradoxes in Roman history.

Augustus was both the first Emperor and the founder of the dynasty that reigned for nearly a century. He managed to consolidate the powers of countless offices and positions. Everything flowed through him. He was the ultimate decision-maker and influencer. Augustus took the powers of Caesar to even loftier heights, and yet, no conspiracy even came close to toppling him. In a city where being accused of kingly ambitions was the same as being denounced for treason, Augustus was king in

The temple in the middle is the Temple of Mars the Avenger—the showpiece of the Forum of Augustus. A careful look at the walls to the right and left show the asymmetry.

every way but name. How did he continue to rule when Caesar was cut down for less?

Augustus's rise to the top didn't happen all at once. It happened by degrees, over time. With each step up the ladder, the Roman people had time to adjust. He, in turn, worked very carefully to maintain the illusion of his deference to traditional institutions. He worked hard to act like he didn't have power precisely so he could maintain it.

When it came time to build his grand forum, Augustus faced a dilemma. The owner of some of the land didn't feel like selling. As the most powerful man in the world, Augustus could have asserted his will. Instead, he chose to have the construction proceed, allowing that his forum would be slightly misshapen. It proved to be a powerful symbol. By showing deference to a private citizen, Augustus demonstrated his respect for the individual and the rule of law. Like so many things in his life and career, it was a façade, an elaborate and carefully maintained façade.

It's subtle, but take your time. From the viewing platform, take in the whole sweep of the Forum of Augustus. Imagine the Emperor marching the steps to the Temple of Mars the Avenger, banners waving in the breeze as he ascends to the sanctuary, flanked by elite soldiers with armor polished to gleam in the bright Italian sun, solemnly offering sacrifice to Mars for another victory, another vanquished foe, another mark of glory in his illustrious reign. But take care to look right and look left. Look at the corners, the sides. It takes a moment to reconstruct the grand plazas in your mind, to see the buildings rise from the ruins. When you take it all in, you'll see the asymmetry. What started for Augustus as an inconvenience of real estate has endured in a 2,000-year-old symbol of how he was seen, and how he wanted to be seen. Augustus circumvented tradition by explicitly paying homage to it.

Address: Via dei Fori Imperiali.

Nearest Metro: Colosseu, Metro Line B. A six to seven-minute walk from both the Metro and the Colosseum.

CHAPTER 5

The Mausoleum of Augustus

After gaining sole control over the Roman world in his early thirties, the man who would come to be known as Augustus got to work on building—what else—his tomb. Talk about a guy with a sense of his own destiny. He would have nearly four decades to admire it before taking occupancy himself. Fortunately, it was worth admiring.

The Mausoleum of Augustus was, and still is, massive. At the time, it was the largest tomb built in Rome. Unfortunately for the first Emperor, he had plenty of occasions to send friends and family to its embrace before he would join them. When his time came in 14 CE, his last words were, "Have I played the part well? Then applaud as I exit." To his dying day, Augustus knew

The Mausoleum under renovation. Maybe the reputation of Caligula will be restored along with it?

his role in public life was all show. In order to maintain absolute power, he had to act like he didn't have any.

His successors would stray from the script. When the divine Augustus finally died, power was transferred to his step-son, Tiberius. He wasn't the first choice, or the second, or third, or fourth, but he eventually got the gig. Tiberius was accomplished as a general and statesman; he held prominent offices and had a first-class education. He generally carried on the tradition of at least pretending to defer to the Senate. But Tiberius also had thin skin, and grew increasingly tired of public life. Eventually, he withdrew to his pleasure palaces on the island of Capri. Tiberius barely feigned interest in events back in Rome. He left his chief bodyguard, Sejanus, in control. Big mistake. Sejanus was ruthless, ambitious, and manipulative. He killed lots of people. He was strutting around like he ran the place while preventing anyone from telling Tiberius about what was really going on.

No matter how withdrawn Tiberius had become, he hadn't closed all channels of communication. Eventually, word got to him that Sejanus was acting the part of Emperor. Tiberius maneuvered to have him arrested, thrown in the Mamertine Prison, and executed. Once that was complete, Tiberius ordered the execution of anyone suspected of being connected to Sejanus. The killing eventually stopped, but Tiberius grew paranoid. He ordered his great nephew Gaius to Capri.

Gaius was the youngest son of Germanicus, himself the son of Tiberius's beloved brother Drussus, who had died after suffering an injury at the frontier. Tiberius was devastated by the loss of his brother, but he had no real affection for his nephew. Germanicus was the most popular man in Rome, charming and handsome, a dashing general with a beautiful young family. To upstage the Emperor was risky, and in due course, Germanicus died in mysterious circumstances. The people were grief-stricken. Tiberius was blamed and his popularity plummeted.

Germanicus's two older sons had been victims of the cycles of purge and recrimination. Now, years later, the youngest was summoned to Capri so Tiberius could keep a close watch. What must have been going through the young man's mind is unimaginable. He was at the mercy of an increasingly paranoid old man, who had a hand in the murder of his siblings and probably his dad.

On Capri, Gaius had a front-row seat to his great uncle's debauched and violent behavior. Very bad things happened on Capri. Tiberius indulged every fantasy, unrestrained from the norms of society. When he grew bored of people, they were thrown off cliffs to their deaths. Very bad things indeed.

To the relief of everyone, Tiberius died in 37 CE. He hadn't set foot in Rome in more than a decade. Unloved and unmourned, Tiberius was quietly interred in the Mausoleum. The people rejoiced as his great nephew Gaius ascended to the throne. Gaius was young, charismatic, and the son of the beloved Germanicus. He even had a snappy nickname: Caligula.

Rome cheered their new Emperor. Caligula was in his early twenties. Everyone heralded the beginning of a long, peaceful, and prosperous era.

At the start of Caligula's reign, that's exactly what they got. He cancelled the political persecutions, recalled exiled citizens, and organized tax reform. He called for festivals and games. Rome was giddy. Then, about six months into the good times, Caligula fell gravely ill. An anxious hush fell over the city. One nervous Senator vowed that he would trade his own life for the stricken young Emperor's. Sacrifices were made, auspices were taken, and then, by the grace of the gods, Caligula recovered. The people rejoiced. And then, things got . . . weird.

Back on his feet, Caligula went on a three-year run of lunacy and debauchery that almost defies belief. He got started by taking the well-intentioned Senator up on his offer, ignoring the obvious rhetoric of his comments. The gentleman who said he would give his life for the

Emperor's was compelled to do so by committing suicide. So much for "it's the thought that counts."

Back in the days of Uncle Tiberius, a fortune teller had made a glib remark that equated Caligula's chances of becoming Emperor with those of his ability to ride a horse across the ocean. Rather than be content that the wacko had been proven wrong, Caligula decided to have his cake and eat it too. He ordered that a miles-long pontoon bridge be built across a bay so he could ride his favorite horse across it. Orders are orders; the bridge was duly built and Caligula performed his stunt. He was pleased with himself. He might have been the only one.

His oceanic escapades extended even further away from the capital. With armies marching all over Europe, Caligula wanted to use Rome's military might to add to his glory. But what fun would it be to defeat mere mortals? Accordingly, Caligula had his armies march to the coast of Gaul (modern France), and attack the beach. The *empty* beach. Following orders, Caligula's men gathered up seashells, which Caligula proudly displayed to prove that he had vanquished the mighty ocean.

Tiberius might have been a weird old guy "working from home" on Capri, but at least he was frugal and pragmatic when it came to cash management. When Caligula took over, the Empire was on sound financial footing. But Caligula's stunts were more than just weird; they were expensive. The coffers were drained and the profligate young Emperor needed cash. What else would he do but turn the imperial palace into a brothel, where the wives of noblemen were forced to perform "service" for the benefit of the Empire?

No one was safe; nothing was sacred. Soldiers were dismissed from the army, just a few days short of retirement, and thus denied their pensions. Senators, whether one was a true enemy or just one in the mind of the Emperor, were ruthlessly tortured and killed. The treason trials of Tiberius, which Caligula had banished to the delight of the people, were resumed. Self-conscious of his male pattern baldness, Caligula made it illegal to look at his head. At one point, he threatened to make his favorite horse a consul. He began to see himself as a god, and insisted that people worship him as such.

Caligula's greatest hits of crazy go on and on. What's surprising is not that someone murdered him, but that it took four years to do it. One January day in 41 CE, while walking in an underground passage beneath the imperial palace, some of the guards fell on Caligula, hacking him to death at the tender age of twenty-eight. Thus died one of history's greatest villains.

Everyone knows Caligula was nuts. But was he?

The historians that give us the account of his life and career all had an axe to grind. By the time he came to power, the pretense of Senatorial influence was pure farce. It was the great unspoken truth, the elephant in the room. Maybe Caligula was crazy. Or maybe the historians that portrayed him as such hated that he laid bare the stark truth: the Senate had no power; the traditional institutions of Rome were a shell. The power of the Emperor was absolute and there was nothing any of them could do about it. What ended up getting Caligula wasn't even a Senatorial conspiracy; it was a group of angry bodyguards that had taken enough of his abuse.

When you consider some of the actions of Caligula, and cast them in a new light, there may be a method to the madness after all. Caligula resented the fakeness of the Roman aristocracy. He was the Emperor and they were sycophants, hanging on to a long-dead system. He knew it. They knew it. He set out to prove it. For example, if Senators truly had no real prestige or influence, didn't appointing his horse as consul prove the point? Consider his insistence that people acknowledge his divinity. Since the rise of Augustus, Senators had griped about the loss of their prestige when the Emperor wasn't around, then tripped over themselves to outdo one another with honors and praise for him when he was. Caligula's proclamations of divinity just shortcut the process. When seen through the lens of a young man trying to expose what he saw as hypocrisy, Caligula's actions become less crazy.

The histories that come down to us from this period were largely written by bookish Senators. They had incentive to cast Caligula as a villain; he had proven them to be powerless and out of date. With the Emperor dead, they could twist stories, exaggerate, and just plain make stuff up. The world has always loved salacious gossip and scurrilous character assassination. The pen is mightier than the sword. For Caligula, however, the sword was pretty mighty too. He got the worse end of both.

Today, the Mausoleum of Augustus is in a state of disrepair. Having been long neglected, the ruins are unstable. However, an ambitious renovation is underway. Financing has been secured and plans have been drawn up. It's very much worth visiting, walking around the perimeter and reflecting on the people it interred: Augustus, Agrippa, Livia, Germanicus, Tiberius, Caligula, and so many others. Despite all the family drama, heartbreak, tragedy, and betrayal, they all ended up in the same place.

This is a building that deserves to be restored. It tells the story of the rise and fall of the family that has some of the most complicated, powerful, weird, and brilliant people ever. Their words and actions altered the course of human history.

As the Mausoleum of Augustus undergoes rehabilitation, there is a murmur that the accepted story of Caligula's life may not match the reality. Time will tell if these whispers become louder. Maybe when the building opens, the reputation of one of history's greatest villains will be restored. Or maybe Caligula really just was that crazy.

In death, we lose control of our reputation and legacy. The judgment of our lives and actions are left to others. The Mausoleum of Augustus is the perfect place to contemplate, to wonder, to ask yourself, "What will people say about me when I'm gone?"

➤ How to get to the Mausoleum of Augustus

The Mausoleum is directly across the street from the Ara Pacis, on the Tiber, in between the Ponte Margherita and the Ponte Cavour. It is a thirty-five-minute walk from the Colosseum and a ten-minute walk from the Spagna Metro station (Line A).

Address: Piazza Augusto Imperatore, Campo Marzio.

➤ Local eats

Discover classic Roman cuisine and seafood in an unpretentious setting:

Il Gabriello ($$)

Via Vittoria 51, 00187

+39 06 6994 0810

www.ilgabriello.com/en/

Get a healthy start with a fresh juice, fruit, or baguette sandwich:

Ginger Sapori e Salute ($$)

Via Borgognona 43-46, 00187

+39 06 6994 0836

www.gingersaporiesalute.com/locations/rome-borgognona

Luxuriate in a Michelin-rated restaurant with a terrific view of the Spanish Steps:

Imago at the Hassler ($$$)

6 Piazza Trinita dei Monti, c/o Hotel Hassler Roma, 00187

+39 06 6993 4726

www.hotelhasslerroma.com/en/restaurants-bars/imago/

➤ **Want more of the story before the next chapter?** *Stop by the Temple of Claudius.*

Take notice during strolls around Rome and you will see lots of oddities. Here and there, large blocks of stone of great antiquity are embedded in walls, as if there is an older building hiding within a more modern one. If you happen to be walking around the Caelian Hill, you can see one such example, where the foundation blocks of the ancient Temple of Claudius are embedded within the bell tower of The Basilica of Saints John and Paul. Claudius is overlooked, and it's appropriate that of all the Emperors, the scant remains of his temple are hiding, almost afraid to be seen.

Succession in the Julio-Claudian dynasty tells of smooth transitions of power from Augustus to Caligula. However, along the way, many in the family died in mysterious circumstances, or were simply eliminated in overt political assassinations. One just wasn't worth the effort. His mother thought he was a monster. He stammered, had a limp, and was partially deaf.

Considered too harmless to be worthy of elimination, Claudius drifted through life in the imperial palace. No one bothered to kill him. No one took him seriously. But in the immediate chaos following the death of Caligula, one of the soldiers found poor Claudius alone in the palace, cowering behind a curtain, trying to avoid the bloodshed. As the uncle of the dead Emperor and the brother of the beloved Germanicus, Claudius was the only one who could conceivably be Emperor. The soldier whisked him away to the barracks, where the troops backed his claim to the throne.

It's likely that the imperial bodyguard advocated his cause because he was considered to be weak-minded; he could be their puppet. Besides, he promised lots of cash to the men. The guy everyone thought was too stupid to become Emperor became Emperor.

Then something amazing happened; Claudius turned out to be . . . good. His family had confused his speech impediment with stupidity and badly misjudged him. He had spent his life neglected, and had withdrawn into reading and writing extensively about history. Scholarly and bookish, he was well-grounded in political philosophy. It seems that he played up his impairments as a calculated move designed to keep safe in the brutal world of palace politics. Once he held the reins of power, Claudius made solid decisions and demonstrated pragmatic administration. He enriched the Empire and added to its social and military glory. Once a laughing stock, Claudius was firmly in control and the Empire was thriving.

Things went south with his fourth marriage. At nearly sixty, he married his niece. Eww. She was twenty-five years his junior. Double eww. More than creepy, his choice was deadly. Calculating and with smoldering ambition, she quietly poisoned her uncle/husband to make room for her son, Nero. To maintain the charade of mourning, mother and son erected a massive temple to the newly deified Claudius.

Very little of it remains today. It's fitting, as history has proven Claudius to be overlooked and underappreciated. These things happen when you're sandwiched between such villains as Caligula and Nero. Such an interesting character deserves a greater imprint in the archaeological record. But you will know something that most people don't: what the stones were, and in whose honor they were erected. Besides, it's appropriate, and a bit ironic. Claudius hid behind a curtain to avoid being seen. What remains of his temple is hiding within a wall, to prevent him from being remembered.

CHAPTER 6

The Colosseum

The Colosseum is the most famous Roman building. Indeed, it's one of the most famous in the world. It's so famous that it's easy to assume that we know everything about it. But even this great building hides a few secrets from the millions of tourists that visit every year.

When huge swaths of Rome went up in flames in the famous Great Fire, the Emperor Nero was out of town. Hearing of the disaster, he rushed to the city and immediately began to oversee relief efforts. The fire took days to burn itself out. When it was done, half the population was homeless. Nero opened gardens and palaces to give people shelter and organized food relief. Had he focused solely on caring for his people, he probably would have been okay. Unfortunately for Nero, he was, well, Nero.

With so much of the city destroyed, Nero's mind turned to rebuilding. Rather than make sure everyone had a home, his biggest focus was himself. He began construction on a huge pleasure palace, the Domus Aurea (Golden House); the place eventually took up about 25 percent of the entire city. That's a big house. It wasn't cheap, either. To fund his passion project, Nero nearly bankrupted the Empire, ratcheting up taxes far and wide. The cash might have come in, but resentment and hostility festered. People started grumbling that maybe Nero had started the fire in the first place. Maybe he just wanted all that land for himself.

Oblivious to the disaffection of his people, Nero kept building. As his palace neared completion, he said: "Now I can at last begin to live like a human being!"

In the middle of the Domus Aurea was a large, man-made lake, with the clever Roman engineers diverting and channeling water in sophisticated ways. Unfortunately for Nero, the people weren't taking time to admire the engineering; they were too busy resenting their home-lessness, hunger, and unemployment. The only person Nero was paying any attention to was Nero. To prove the point, next to the lake he had a giant statue of himself erected. Nearly one hundred feet tall, the statue was a monument to Nero's glory. Or ego. Or both. Little could he know that soon, the statue would be the only thing that remained of his pleasure palace and that his reign was reaching a dramatic and violent end.

Taxed into oblivion to underwrite Nero's narcissism, the people of the Empire had enough. A general in a far-away province rebelled and began to march on Rome. Nero's advisors, bodyguards, and servants fled before the coming storm. Before he could be deposed, Nero committed suicide. At the fateful moment, a hesitant, and still very much out-of-touch Nero said: "What an artist the world is losing."

Nero had reigned for thirteen years, and was the last ruler of the famed Julio-Claudians, the dynasty that started with Julius Caesar one hundred years earlier. The new guy, Galba, was a well-respected governor and administrator. But if the citizens were hoping for relief from the chaos of Nero's final years, they were to be seriously disappointed. Galba was a humorless stiff with no ability to connect with people. He didn't last a year. He was murdered and replaced by Otho.

Otho had been Nero's drinking buddy until the Emperor developed eyes for his friend's wife, Poppaea Sabina. Accordingly, Nero had "promoted" Otho to be governor to a faraway province to have the lovely lady to himself. Otho had surprised everyone by being a moderate and decent governor. Nero surprised no one by being a vicious megalomaniac. When the pregnant Poppaea—now his wife—nagged him about spending too much time at the races, he kicked her so hard in the abdomen that not only did she lose the baby, but she died as well. Now, all these years later, Otho was the man.

With so much turnover, all sorts of people got ideas about being in charge. While Otho was strutting his stuff, another general—Vitellius—rose up in rebellion and marched on the capital. Just three months into his reign, Otho was defeated in battle and promptly committed suicide. Vitellius settled in to a long and prosperous reign. Of eight months.

Yet another general had been watching and waiting. Vespasian hadn't thrown himself into the mix at the beginning. While the other contenders took turns knocking each other off, Vespasian and his trusted son/ chief lieutenant Titus were in Judea, fighting the First Roman-Jewish War. Emperor after Emperor rose and fell. Vespasian decided it was time to make his move. He set off for Rome, leaving Titus in charge. The in- fighting had left all the factions reasonably weak, and Vespasian didn't have much trouble grabbing the impe- rial throne and putting an end to what has come to be known as the "Year of Four Emperors." Nero, Galba,

Otho, Vitellius—all dead. Vespasian wanted stability and needed legitimacy.

He needed to show the people of Rome that he was a benefactor, nothing like those hedonists and incompetents that had come before him. This was the beginning of a new era. The Julio-Claudians were gone and the pretenders had been cast aside. His ambition was sweeping, but his vision was, well, expensive, but cash was on short supply.

Back in Judea, Titus was about to bring his siege of Jerusalem to a dramatic conclusion. On August 30th, 70 CE, Titus breached the defensive walls and his army poured into the city. The soldiers raped, pillaged, and destroyed, sacking the holy city and looting its treasures. The biggest prize for the Romans was the Second Temple, the holiest sanctuary for the Jews, and home of great treasure. The Romans carted off the riches and razed the Temple. All that remains of the once great building is the Western Wall, or Wailing Wall. To this day, it is a location of prayer and deep lamentation. The Romans chose a different way to observe the outcome.

Flush with cash, Titus marched in glory back to Rome. For his accomplishments, he was awarded a Triumph. Titus and Vespasian readied to make their mark on Rome, and on the hearts and minds of the citizens. They wanted to proclaim the glory of their new-founded

Everyone knows this building,
but where does it get its name?

Flavian dynasty, to show the people they were different, better. They began to build.

With the plunder from Jerusalem financing their grand vision, construction on the Flavian Amphitheater began in earnest. In a good PR move, he used much of the land from the Domus Aurea, in particular, the big man-made lake. The engineers drained the lake and laid the cornerstone for their massive entertainment complex.

And that's what the Colosseum is: a giant piece of imperial propaganda. A building for the ages, a declaration of the eternal and everlasting glory of the Flavians, built with the spoils of war from the sack of Jerusalem. Of course, no one calls the building the Flavian Amphitheater today. Call it that, and you're likely to be met with blank stares.

Call it the Colosseum, though, and everyone will know *exactly* what you are talking about. So why didn't the "official" name stick, and why was it replaced with "Colosseum"?

Remember that giant statue of Nero? Vespasian's builders had pulled down the walls of the Domus Aurea, and drained the lake to reclaim land for their project. But they left the statue standing. Nero's homage to himself—roughly the size of the Statue of Liberty—had been modeled on the Colossus of Rhodes. Why would

Vespasian leave intact a statue to his disgraced predecessor? He didn't leave it exactly intact. Vespasian had the head lopped off and replaced with a representation of his own. The Colossus of Nero became the Colossus of Vespasian. It didn't matter that they bore little physical resemblance to one another. Nero had the statue built to resemble the physique of a god; Vespasian was fine with that. With a new head, the statue was good to go.

Through the years, as Emperors came and went, off went one head and on came another. But the statue remained. That's where the name comes from, the Colossus of Nero, Vespasian, whomever. After a while, the name became a useful landmark and was easier than "Flavian Amphitheater." The name stuck and endured for centuries, far longer than the memory of many of the people whom it featured.

As you stand outside the Colosseum, consider that the ground under your feet was once underwater, submerged under Nero's artificial lake. Remember that the project was developed with treasure ripped away from the sacked Jerusalem, and that after the bloodshed and chaos of the Year of Four Emperors, a new dynasty rose to add stability to the fractious Empire. Meditate on the transient nature of fame and power, on all the great and powerful rulers whose names and lives are relegated to the footnotes of history. And in a quiet moment, remember Nero. As you navigate the throngs of tourists, imagine the Domus Aurea and his great lake. Tune out the noise and bustle of the modern world and walk in the private pleasure palace of one history's greatest villains. Imagine a statue, soaring nearly one hundred feet above the ground and smile because you know; the statue is long gone, but its name lives on, even if no one else seems to be in on the secret.

➤ How to get to the Colosseum

The Colosseum is the easiest building in Rome to find! Just follow the crowds or ask anyone to point the way. It's directly across from the Colosseo Metro station (Line B).

Address: Piazza del Colosseo.

➤ Hours

Hours vary. The Colosseum generally opens at 8:30 a.m. It's largely the closing times that are variable. The earliest it closes is 4:30 p.m., but between March and late August, it may be open as late as 7:15 p.m. Check the following website for up-to-date hours, and given that it is the most popular attraction in Rome, consider buying tickets in advance. Prepare for long entry lines.

For more information, visit *www.turismoroma.it /cosa-fare/colosseo-2?lang=en*.

➤ Local eats

Be amazed at how good carry-out meatballs can be:
ALLbiBOX ($)
Largo Corrado Ricci 34, Fori Imperiali, 00184 Rome
+39 06 9784 1165
www.allbibox.com/

Re-energize with good and reasonably priced sandwiches in the shadow of the Colosseum:
Pane & Vino ($)
Via Ostilia 10, 00184
+39 06 7720 7177
www.facebook.com/colosseopanevino

Get your chocolate fix; vegan and gluten-free options available:
Grezzo Raw Chocolate ($)
Via Urbana 130, 00184
+39 06 483443
https://grezzorawchocolate.com/

Leave your mark in a spot where customers can graffiti the walls:

La Carbonara ($$)
Via Panisperna 214, 00184
+39 06 482 5176
www.lacarbonara.it/

➤ Want more of the story before the next chapter? *Stop by the Arch of Titus.*

The Forum can be overwhelming. Some buildings still stand; others are completely ruined. No matter where you are, the palpable sense of standing in the beating heart of the mighty Roman Empire is a constant reminder of the gravity of the events that happened in this place. Amidst the ruins, one building seems to puff its chest out, proudly standing sentinel. It continued the Roman tradition of using buildings as propaganda to convey legitimacy. It also emblazons in marble the story of an emotional scar in the psyche of millions of people.

Financed by the spoils of war, the Colosseum proved that the new ruling family, the Flavians, had the people's interests at heart. Nero had bankrupted the Empire for his own enjoyment. Now, thanks to the benevolence of the Flavians, the people could enjoy the bloody spectacle

The Arch of Titus.

Detail shows Titus looking down from heaven, at the top center of the underside of the arch.

of gladiator shows and animal fights. The engineers even used the plumbing from Nero's private lake to great effect, allowing the Colosseum to be flooded for naval battles, yet another hidden legacy of Nero's megalomania.

Vespasian died of natural causes in 69 CE. Given the Romans' tendency to posthumously deify their emperors, he is said to have joked on his deathbed, "I fear I am turning into a god!" It was left to his son Titus to both run the Empire and open the Colosseum.

Maybe they were insecure about their somewhat humble origins, but they didn't stop at the Colosseum, erecting the Arch of Titus to laud his martial achievements. It was a beautiful monument, built by Titus's younger brother Domitian after Titus's untimely death, and demonstrated to the people that the gods continued to favor the Flavians.

This hulking arch stands almost arrogantly in the heart of the Forum, proclaiming the everlasting glory of the Flavians.

It also tells a darker story—the story of a decimated people and the destruction of their most sacred place. To the Romans, the sack of Jerusalem had been a glorious accomplishment. But to the Jews, the destruction of the Temple was cataclysmic. While the Romans paraded their victories, hundreds of generations of Jews have mourned the loss of their sacred relics, the devastation of the great temple, and the violation of their most holy sanctuary.

Go to the arch. Look up. In the middle of the underside, the sculpture depicts Titus looking down from heaven as a god, joining his dad in the pantheon. With a couple of Flavians looking down from heaven, and Domitian in charge down on earth, the Empire was in great hands.

But let your eyes come down from the top to the side of the arch and the story begins to change.

Find the depiction of the sack of the Temple of Jerusalem. Clear as day you can see the holy menorah being carted off to Rome, doomed to be melted down for cash. The contrast is stark. The treasures seized by the Roman military may have paid for the construction of the most famous of all Roman buildings, but they also underwrote the ever-complicated legacy of the Roman Empire.

Address: Roman Forum.

Nearest Metro: Colosseo, Metro Line B. A three-to-four-minute walk from both the Metro and the Colosseum.

—— CHAPTER 7 ——

Piazza Navona

In the complicated history of Rome, sometimes what's not there is as telling as what is.

No trip to Rome would be complete without a trip to Piazza Navona. It's is a Renaissance masterpiece, complete with elegant buildings and sublime fountains. There are cafes and street artists; the whole area has a festive feel. But stand there long enough, and you will start to get a vague notion of the strange shape of the Piazza. It is oblong, elliptical, and odd for a public space. The story of the shape of the piazza is interesting, and an apt-metaphor for the life, death, and legacy of Rome's 11th Emperor.

When Vespasian died in 79 CE, people were bummed out, but at least they knew he was turning things over to his talented oldest son, Titus. Considered a hero in his

The length of the piazza.

own right, Titus's fame and popularity were vast. He was a victorious general, a capable administrator, and a moderate ruler. He was charming, strong, and handsome—perfect to secure the family fortunes for generations. All he needed was to find himself a wife and have male heirs. He was the most eligible bachelor in the Empire.

What could possibly go wrong?

Rome being Rome, the good times couldn't last. In the first year of Titus's reign, Mount Vesuvius erupted, destroying cities such as Pompeii and Herculaneum. Titus rushed to the area to orchestrate relief efforts. Although the tragedy was undeniable, the people greatly appreciated his zeal for their well-being.

In the second year of his rule, fire ravaged the capital. Again, Titus poured himself into relief efforts.

The Flavians might have vaulted to the top of Roman society, but they had middle-class roots, and a streak of humility unusual for such powerful people. Once, when realizing a whole day had passed without doing anyone a favor, Titus said, "Friends, I have wasted a day." He needed an even keel. The twin disasters of Vesuvius and the fire made the first two years of his reign a true test of character.

And if that wasn't enough, he up and died in his early forties, barely two years into his reign. All of a sudden, the Flavian grip on power was tenuous. Titus had no son, and the last member of the ruling family was his much-overlooked younger brother, Domitian. He was duly crowned Emperor, but many cast a suspicious eye on the untested and unknown youth. While Vespasian had poured all his hopes and ambitions into his dashing oldest son, he had neglected his younger. Domitian had grown up isolated and lonely, in the margins, on his own. Suddenly, with no experience and no relationship with the people, he was the Emperor of Rome.

What could possibly go *right?*

Like his father and brother before him, Domitian needed legitimacy. He needed to remind his people of his family's accomplishments. Titus had begun a temple to the deified Vespasian; he had indeed become a god after all. Domitian added Titus to the project, but that would take years to complete.

He needed a piece of imperial propaganda fast. Military victory was the most highly valued accomplishment in Rome. To vanquish foes and shower Rome with glory showed the favor of the gods. Luckily for Domitian, he came from a family with plenty of such glory, even if he didn't have any of his own. He quickly began a construction project, one that would remind everyone of the great military feats of his illustrious family. After all, if his dad and brother were so great, then he must be too, right? The family already had the Colosseum to its credit. Domitian would add another great monument. And where better to build a monument to family glory than in the very heart of Roman public life: the Forum? Domitian's architects and sculptors converged on the Forum, and in short order, the Arch of Titus rose in triumph. He gained a tentative toe-hold on power. To build momentum, he took on many other ambitious projects.

Carrying on the family tradition of commissioning grand entertainment facilities, Domitian added a new stadium for the benefit and amusement of the Roman people. Some of Rome's notable facilities, the Circus Maximus and the Colosseum, for example, were simply too big for athletic contests like foot races. Although it wasn't the biggest building in Rome, it filled an important need, and 15,000–20,000 Romans would flock to the stadium to take in the games, or *agones* in Latin. The propaganda worked; the people grew fond of the new Emperor, but the Senate was not impressed.

In the rise of Domitian, we see shadows of the rise of Augustus: a young but largely unknown member of a prominent family, who had been overshadowed by more powerful and charismatic relatives. Domitian certainly made the connection, and he set to emulate the great man, styling himself "The New Augustus."

Despite being neglected as a youth, Domitian was a surprisingly competent Emperor. Looking back in history, he studied the works and policies of Augustus, using the first Emperor as a guidepost. Domitian understood that Augustus had laid out the blueprint: strengthen the borders and defenses and eschew expansion. He also followed the Augustan game plan by improving infrastructure, building, and beautifying the city. Where Augustus could boast that he found Rome a city of brick and left it a city of marble, Domitian could claim to have provided Rome with his own renewal, building on the foundation of the Augustan legacy.

But Domitian missed the most important leadership lessons from Augustus: the need to manage the egos and perceptions of the people around him. Where Augustus was happy working in the background, Domitian was impatient with those who did not fall in line. Augustus subtly guided policy with a discreet but unwavering hand. Domitian was a true command-and-control autocrat. Augustus slowly marginalized opponents, and discretely steered power toward his favorites. Domitian exiled or murdered those who stood in his way. Augustus died a peaceful death well past his life expectancy, beloved by the people. Domitian lived in fear of assassins.

A prophecy foretold that Domitian would die around noon. Paranoid of assassination, every day he would lock himself away and wait for the dreaded hour to pass. Only once he knew that it was safely past noon would he reemerge and get back to work.

Eventually, the conspiracy that he feared came to pass. Planning in advance, a member of the palace staff faked an arm injury so that everyone, Domitian included, would get used to the bandages on his arm, perfect for concealing a dagger.

On the fateful day, Domitian asked the time, as was his custom. A servant lied, stating that it was later in the day than it actually was. Letting his guard down, Domitian emerged from his solitude ready to get back to work when the assassins struck. He was strong and fought for his life, but he was eventually overpowered and cut down. He bled to death on the floor of the imperial palace, dying around noon: the hour the prophecy had foretold. He was forty-five.

After the deed was done, the Senate sought their revenge on the fallen Emperor. They damned Domitian's memory and sought to purge his name from the histories. They toppled his statues and melted down his coins, trying to wipe out the memory of Domitian, as though he had never existed. It didn't matter that he had been a competent ruler. It didn't matter that his policies were good, pragmatic, and effective. Domitian had sought to emulate Augustus, but he only looked at part of the picture. Policy was not enough. Domitian missed that becoming "The New Augustus" required a great *performance*. Perception mattered as much as policy. For nearly 2,000 years, the reputation of Domitian has been sullied by the hatred toward him in his own time.

Today, Domitian doesn't garner much attention. His name isn't commonly known, and the buildings of his family that do remain carry the names of his illustrious father and brother. But his shadow looms in Rome, and in Piazza Navona, it looms large, which owes its odd shape to the murdered Emperor.

The Piazza is the site of the Stadium of Domitian. With time, the word *agones*, "games," slowly morphed into *navona*. Thus: Piazza Navona. Through the centuries, the stadium fell to ruins. Many of its stones were carted off to become part of new buildings. Eventually, all that remained of Domitian's stadium was the outline of the track. The piazza that you see today owes its shape to this forgotten stadium; the buildings trace the outline of the structure.

No matter where you stand in the piazza, look around. With only a little imagination, you can see yourself standing on the floor of the Stadium of Domitian. The Senate may have damned his memory, but he is still there. It was an appropriate transformation: from the neglected youth hiding in the shadows of a famous father and older brother, to the assassinated Emperor, hiding in the shadows of one of Rome's grand piazzas. All that remains might be a shadow, but if you look just right, you can still see him, and together, you can have the last laugh on a Senate that tried to wipe the memory of Domitian away.

➤ How to get to Piazza Navona

Piazza Navona is northwest from the Forum, a thirty-minute walk from the Colosseum and a twenty-minute walk from the Barberini Metro station (Line A). It's a lively, festive area, with lots of local dining options. The piazza is a public space, open around the clock. At the north end, there is an underground museum, with what little archaeology of the stadium remains. It's worth a visit.

Address: Piazza Navona.

➤ Local eats

Cool off with a great gelato:
La Gelateria Frigidarium ($)
Via del Governo Vecchio 112, 00186
+39 334 995 1184
www.frigidarium-gelateria.com/

Start the day with a great breakfast in a relaxed atmosphere:
Coromandel ($$)
Via Di Monte Giordano 60/61, 00186
+39 06 6880 2461
www.coromandel.it/

Unwind with a glass of wine in a relaxed café:
Etabli ($$)
Vicolo delle Vacche 9, 00186
+39 06 9761 6694
www.etabli.it/

Hang with locals in a bar with a lively late-night scene:
Bar del Fico ($$)
Piazza del Fico, 26–28, Via Della Pace 34, 00187
+39 06 6889 1373
www.bardelfico.com/en/

➤ Want more of the story before the next chapter? *Stop by Trajan's Column.*

Roman history is fascinating for its twists and turns. Leaders rose and fell. Armies were victorious then vanquished. Buildings were erected then toppled. One monument in the Forum tells a great story, quite literally through its twists and turns.

After the death of Domitian, the old Senator and statesman Nerva was proclaimed Emperor. He was a good administrative choice, but lacked charisma. The people were underwhelmed. Nerva had a simple plan to gain the affection of the people, and ensure his own safety: Adopt the most popular man in the Empire. Walking down the street one day, Nerva yelled out: "I adopt Trajan!" That was it. Done deal. No paperwork necessary. To off Nerva would mean the people would lose the chance of having their favorite inherit the Empire. Nerva would enjoy the security until his dying day, a few months later.

Trajan was a dashing general, leading his armies to victory after victory. When Nerva died, the energetic Trajan didn't sit back and enjoy the desk job of Emperor; he kept fighting. Trajan stacked up piles of victories, cementing the love and adulation of the people. Like

Trajan's Column.

many before, he began to build. His grand building program changed the face of Rome.

Trajan's engineers moved mountains . . . well, hills. The sides of the Quirinal and Capitoline hills were leveled to create space for a massive new forum and market complex. Trajan's Market added to the city's economic activity. He added the last of the Imperial Forums, and in the middle, Trajan erected a column to mark his martial accomplishments over the barbarians of far-off Dacia.

The innovative column used sculpture, carved in relief, to proclaim the glory of the god-like Trajan. The sculpture wraps its way around the column, with thousands of figures engaged in the epic struggle. With each turn around the column, the military continues its relentless march toward victory. By the top, enemies have been vanquished, the Empire enriched, and Trajan victorious.

The column is a can't miss. The stories it tells are fascinating. The exquisite sculpture gives a detailed account of Roman military tactics and weaponry, invaluable for historians. As far as imperial propaganda goes, it couldn't be beat. Although the column is ninety-eight feet tall, the winding frieze afforded Trajan 600 linear feet of sculpture to tell the story of the might of Rome. But it couldn't climb forever.

The column could only be so high, and the story the frieze told was finite. It had an end. As did Rome's expansion. The further the Empire expanded, the longer the borders and the greater their distance from the capital. After a while, the pull of gravity would be too great and the borders would contract.

The Column of Trajan represents the military accomplishments of its builder, as intended, and represents the peak of Roman power. But the deeper meaning, one that requires a closer consideration, is the meaning and nature of Empire. When Trajan died a few years after the column's completion, the inevitable pull of gravity began tugging the borders back. The Empire had hit its apex. The long, slow decline of the Western Empire had begun.

Address: Trajan's Forum (via the Roman Forum).

Nearest Metro: Colosseo, Metro Line B. A ten-to-twelve-minute walk from both the Metro and the Colosseum.

CHAPTER 8

The Pantheon

The façade of the world's most perfectly preserved ancient temple is emblazoned with a lie or, perhaps, a half-truth. Either way, it's misleading.

The inscription is in Latin, and the Romans often wrote in shorthand, so readers knew, for example, that "COS" meant "Consul." Once you know what you're looking for, the words across the front of the Pantheon say, "Marcus Agrippa, son of Lucius, built this when consul for the third time."

By the time the majestic building was completed, the great Agrippa had been dead for more than a century and a quarter. So clearly, he didn't build it. But if he didn't, then who did? And why did they attribute the masterpiece to someone else? These are answers worth knowing; whether you look down at the magnificent porphyry and marble floor, up at the coffered dome, or anywhere in between, you are rewarded with an awe-inspiring tableau.

The story of the Pantheon is, like so many buildings in Rome, both complicated and fun. But the Pantheon is more than a beautiful building. It's more than the people who built it. It is an enduring symbol of the genius of the Romans, and their constant ability to innovate, break new ground, and do the impossible.

The original Pantheon was indeed built by our old friend Agrippa. Considering Agrippa's humble family origins, his rise to the top of the Roman world was remarkable. Building a grand temple with his name carved across the façade would be a great way to preserve his legacy.

But Agrippa's Pantheon was nothing like the building that now stands. Archaeology of the original plan is scant, as Agrippa's temple was destroyed by fire on or before 80 CE. Either way, by the time Domitian was succeeding his short-lived brother Titus, he was looking for ways to prove the stability of the family. Always an enthusiastic builder, Domitian restored the building. Fire, always a dire threat in any ancient city, struck again in 110 CE and the building was again ruined. Devastating though they were, the upshot of big fires was that an Emperor could clear land and build. Lucky for Trajan, he had an ace in the hole, one of the geniuses of antiquity: his chief architect/engineer, Apollodorus of Damascus.

When Trajan had wanted to conquer the territory on the far side of the Danube, Apollodorus designed and built a stone bridge across which Trajan's armies could go a-conquerin'. At two thirds of a mile long and nearly fifty feet wide, it was an efficient way to extend the might of Rome, and a staggering achievement of engineering. It was 1,000 years before a longer bridge was built. The tribes didn't have time to marvel over the engineering; they were too busy fighting to defend their homes. They lost. In the ensuing campaign, Trajan grabbed ever-more territory for Rome. Of great significance is that this land, called Dacia, was rich in gold mines. The coffers of the Empire were stuffed and the people across the Empire partied, with celebrations lasting 123 straight days. (Seriously, did these people *ever* work?)

Trajan and Apollodorus teamed up to redesign large swaths of the city, adding Trajan's Forum and marketplace, and erecting Trajan's Column. The dynamic duo also got scheming on a new temple, one that would reflect the glory of Rome and its undefeated Emperor. Together, they turned to the Pantheon, twice gutted by fire and ready for another makeover. Plans were drawn up; land was cleared; work begun.

While all the building was going on, Trajan set his sights on his next conquest. Rome's rival empire was the Parthians to the east. For centuries, the two great empires slugged it out. It was the Parthians that defeated Crassus. It was the Parthians that Caesar had been planning to head off to fight. If Trajan could best Rome's arch-rival once and for all, then his legacy as a great conqueror would be secure. He marched off on campaign while the building in Rome marched relentlessly on.

Trajan's timing was impeccable; just as he was invading, the Parthians were dealing with their own internal political struggles. They just couldn't match the energy, discipline, and resources of the Roman invaders, and Trajan eventually captured the Parthian capital and forced their capitulation. He began the journey back to Rome, ready to celebrate his crowning achievement, but disaster struck when he suffered a stroke on the way home. He didn't have any children, and hadn't seriously considered the issue of his succession. His wife declared that as he lay dying, Trajan had announced his adoption of Hadrian, a distant cousin and a part of the inner court. Hadrian was a well-respected general, savvy administrator, and had the support of the army. What history may never reveal is whether or not Trajan actually named Hadrian as heir, or if his wife just claimed so out of affection. Who would challenge the word of the grieving Empress?

Whether it was Trajan or his wife who made the choice, it was a good one. Hadrian was energetic and intelligent. Rather than sit back and luxuriate in imperial honors, he traveled, visiting all the provinces. Emulating Augustus, he spent as much time on the road as he did in Rome.

As Emperor, Hadrian confronted a paradox. He was generally inclined toward peace. Unlike many of his predecessors, he considered stability, not expansion, to be the ideal. However, without battles to fight, armies could get restless and their commanders could get ideas, a dangerous threat to power. Accordingly, Hadrian put his men to work, ordering constant drilling and war games. More than anything, he had them build. Under his orders, garrisons in the provinces built fortifications across the Empire. The most famous of these is Hadrian's Wall, which spans seventy-three miles across the entire width of Britain.

With stability and governance in mind, Hadrian made the controversial decision to withdraw from Trajan's Parthian conquests. This would evoke criticism,

The exterior of the Pantheon; note the inscription.

and for all his accomplishments, Hadrian could be thin skinned.

Early in his reign, four prominent Senators of high ranking were "discovered" to be plotting against him and executed without trial. This did nothing to endear Hadrian to the nobility, and the relationship between him and Rome's elite was strained. It wasn't good for anyone's health to be seen as a rival to the Emperor. Hadrian's vindictive streak didn't just extend to would-be rivals; in fact, even simply making fun of Hadrian could be a life or death proposition.

Hadrian was a cultured and learned man. He studied extensively, and promoted the arts and learning. Under his rule, culture flourished. He amassed extensive sculptural collections for admiration and made sure his villa was complete with gardens and reflecting pools for quiet contemplation. Deeply enamored of Greece's intellectual legacy, he promoted Athens, supporting its cultural institutions and advocating its importance as a center of learning. He got so wrapped up in the idea of artistry that he even tried his own hand at art and architecture.

By many accounts, he was gifted. But one person wasn't terribly impressed. Hadrian designed the massive Temple of Venus and Roma, which would become the largest temple in ancient Rome. Apollodorus mocked the Emperor's efforts. For all his genius, he should have known this was a bad idea.

Apollodorus had been working on the magnificent rebuild of the Pantheon. The size and scope of the building presented unique challenges. For example, the massive dome was too heavy without some adjustments to building techniques. The clever Apollodorus addressed this in several ways. For one, the dome gets thinner and uses increasingly light materials as it rises, making it lighter with each foot. Additionally, the ceiling is coffered, which certainly adds to the beauty of the interior, but consider how much material was not needed by using this technique. With each set of concentric squares, more weight was eliminated. But above all, the most notable engineering feature is the oculus, the circular hole in the roof. It allows for the weight of the dome to press against itself from all sides, creating strength and stability. Standing in the Pantheon and looking up at the opening, it appears small, but this is an illusion created by the size of the building. The oculus is almost thirty feet across.

As the Pantheon project moved along, Hadrian decided he no longer needed the engineer-in-chief. With Apollodorus's ridicule ringing in his ears, Hadrian had him banished, then executed. Making fun of Hadrian was a bad idea indeed.

The original Emperor that had issued the building commission was gone. Now the architect was too. As was the prerogative of any Emperor, Hadrian could put his stamp on the Pantheon. By right, it was his to claim. Once it was completed, all that was left was to dedicate the magnificent temple with an inscription. Unlike many of his predecessors, who claimed the building projects of others as their own, Hadrian instead gave the credit to someone else entirely. But it wasn't to Trajan, or Apollodorus. Rather, Hadrian had the façade chiseled with a tip of the hat to Marcus Agrippa, the original builder of the first temple to occupy the site. Given Hadrian's prideful insecurity about his artistic merits, and the fact that anyone else who could lay claim to the building was dead, it makes one wonder why Hadrian didn't take credit and inscribe the building with his own name. By evoking the great Agrippa, Hadrian was proclaiming his connection to the Augustan regime, and thus, the glory that came with it.

The Pantheon is unique in that it remained largely intact through the medieval period and Renaissance, through the World Wars, and into today. It has had a life of its own long past the ultimate collapse of the western Roman Empire in 476 CE. Today, the Pantheon is consecrated as a Catholic church. Kings and Queens are

The oculus, thirty feet across, and coffered ceiling.

interred within its walls, as is the great artist Raphael. From the complex, polytheistic Roman gods, to the God of the Catholics, the Pantheon has served as a place of worship for millennia, interrupted only occasionally by fire, rebuilding, or restoration. But no matter how anyone defines their faith, to walk through the portico, through the massive doors, and onto the marble floor, to gaze up at the soaring dome and through the oculus, the experience of the Pantheon is truly spiritual.

After visiting the Pantheon, be sure to step outside and turn around one last time. Find the inscription. It's easy enough to spot "M. Agrippa." What's harder is knowing why it's there in the first place.

➤ How to get to the Pantheon

The Pantheon is northwest of the Forum, and about two blocks due east of Piazza Navona. It is a fifteen-minute walk from the Barberini Metro station (Line A), and a twenty-five-minute walk from the Colosseum.

Address: Piazza della Rotonda - 00186 Roma

Phone number: +39 06 6830 0230

➤ Hours

Monday to Saturday from 9:00 a.m. to 7:30 p.m.
Sunday from 9:00 a.m. to 6:00 p.m.
Closed December 25 and January 1

➤ Local eats

Refresh yourself with a sweet iced granita, or reenergize with coffee:
La Casa del Caffe Tazza d'Oro ($)
Via Degli Orfani 84, 00186
+39 06 678 9792
www.tazzadorocoffeeshop.com/

Dig into a burger and a beer at a casual pub:
Open Baladin ($$)
Via degli specchi, 6 (zona Campo de' Fiori), 00186
+39 06 683 8989
www.openbaladinroma.it/?lang=en

Relish tradition at a long-standing restaurant with classic fare:
Da Armando al Pantheon ($$)
Salita De' Crescenzi 31, 00186
+39 06 6880 3034
www.armandoalpantheon.it/

➤ More information

www.turismoroma.it/cosa-fare/pantheon?lang=en

➤ Want more of the story before the next chapter? *Stop by the Temple of Antoninus and Faustina.*

History is written by the victors. Christianity's rise meant Roman paganism's decline. In some cases, church elders didn't want to re-write history, but erase it altogether. Sometimes it worked, but sometimes, ancient monuments held on just long enough.

The issue of succession troubled Hadrian. His own accession had been tenuous. Some historians think that Trajan had never even chosen Hadrian at all. He knew that to avoid the issue was to tempt the fates and invite civil war.

When it came time to pick a successor, Hadrian made what people thought was a terrible choice, picking a guy with no discernible talent. Hadrian got bailed out when his chosen successor died a few months later. Perhaps breathing a sigh of relief, Hadrian started over. He had taken notice of a very serious, scholarly, and intelligent aristocrat and began scheming. There was only one problem: He was just a teenager.

*The Temple of Antoninus and Faustina showing
the grooves cut into the tops of the columns.*

History had shown what happened when young rulers with no experience took over. Remember Nero and Caligula? Accordingly, Hadrian hatched a plan. He would adopt a well-respected, experienced aristocrat named Antoninus. He, in turn, would adopt the talented young teenager. For good measure, Antoninus would also adopt the natural son of the deceased first heir. Few people remember him, Lucius, but just about everyone has heard of the talented one, Marcus Aurelius. Marcus was smart and learned quickly. When his time came, he would be ready.

But Antoninus just kept living, his long reign eventually stretching to nearly twenty-three blissful years. By many accounts, the reign of Antoninus was the height of Roman peace and prosperity, the apex of Roman culture.

Antoninus outlived his wife Faustina, whom he adored. After her death, he had her deified and a temple built in her honor. When his own long life came to an end, the grateful people added him to the Roman pantheon and the temple was rededicated to include Antoninus.

And there it stood, in the Forum, for hundreds of years, until a group of church leaders decided that a pagan temple had no place in the Christian world. They planned its demolition. Ropes were tied around its columns, and teams of draught animals yoked up. They pulled and pulled. The columns stood firm. After considering their options, they decided to weaken the structural integrity of the columns by cutting big notches in them. This duly done, they tried again. Still nothing. Scarred up though they were, the sturdy columns held.

The demolition men shrugged their shoulders, and chalked up their inability to divine will. A cross was added to the roof; the temple was rechristened as the church San Lorenzo in Miranda. One of antiquity's temples escaped destruction and carried forward for another millennium.

Stand outside the temple/church; look up to the top of the massive columns of the portico. You will see the series of grooves. This was where a battle between pagan and monotheism was fought to a draw. Maybe it was one last act of defiance of the fading Roman gods. Perhaps it was the Christian god who wanted another church among the hundreds sprouting up across the Eternal City. Either way, the building lives on for all to admire.

Address: Roman Forum.

Nearest Metro: Colosseo, Metro Line B. An eight-minute walk from both the Metro and the Colosseum.

CHAPTER 9

The Baths of Caracalla

Imagine two young children sitting in the back of the family car. They have drawn an imaginary line across the seat and argue about whether or not their sibling has crossed it. For countless parents, this is a scenario that plays out often. The image is repeated on TV shows, commercials, and movies. It's common behavior. But it isn't just limited to children in the modern age. Sometimes, even Roman Emperors did it. There can be great comfort in knowing that some things never change. When children argue over imaginary turf, it ranges from frustrating to amusing. When sole control of the Roman Empire is at stake, such arguments could be deadly.

For a while, Rome had a pretty good run in terms of Emperors. The roughly hundred-year sequence of Nerva, Trajan, Hadrian, Antoninus Pius, and Marcus

Aurelius has come to be known as "the five good Emperors." The first four adopted their successors, helping ensure a qualified successor. Then Marcus Aurelius had to tempt the fates and appoint his son, Commodus, as successor.

After the golden age of wise and moderate rulers, Commodus ushers in an era of crazy. Many people know of Commodus because of his portrayal in the movie *Gladiator*. If anything, the movie undersold just how nuts this guy was. He liked to be depicted wearing a lion skin and carrying a big club, in emulation of his hero Hercules. He seemed to think that he was the actual reincarnation of mythology's greatest strongman. He renamed the army, the navy, even Rome itself, in his name. He gave himself a ridiculous, twelve-part name, and renamed the months of the calendar accordingly. And yes, he fought as a gladiator in the Colosseum. Not everyone was enamored of Commodus as he was of himself. After a bizarre reign of twelve years, Commodus was finally offed in 192 CE. Few people mourned; many saw opportunity.

The imperial bodyguards, the Praetorian Guard, were the only armed soldiers allowed in Rome, giving them tremendous power. For new Emperors, it was sound policy to give the Praetorians cash bribes to ensure loyalty.

*The ruins of the Baths of Caracalla. Up close,
they are impressive and offer a tantalizing
glimpse of their former grandeur.*

They could make or break an Emperor. With Commodus dead, they saw dollar signs.

When the new guy Pertinax took office, he had the temerity to implement much-needed reforms. After a few months, the guard got tired of his stingy moralizing and lopped his head off. It didn't matter that Pertinax was competent; all the Praetorians cared about was money. Since they really held the keys to the kingdom, they decided to be proactive. Why not accelerate the process, get another Emperor, and trigger the next loyalty payment?

In a low point in Roman history, the Praetorians held an auction. Two contenders went down to the barracks and bid for the job of Emperor; the highest promised bonus would win the bidder the job. The "winner," Didius Julianus, was crowned in exchange for a huge cash payment to each of the guards. How far had the Empire fallen.

Nonplussed, generals off in the provinces revolted, marching toward Rome and each another. Civil war was at hand again.

In a series of maneuvers, betrayals, and murders, one claimant after another rose and fell. Poor Julianus, who wasn't really a bad guy, was murdered after his body guard decided it was easier to switch sides than get in shape and actually guard his body. This series of contests would go down as the Year of Five Emperors. When the dust settled, one man was left in sole control.

Septimius Severus was a career soldier, politician, and bureaucrat. As with Vespasian, his ascension would establish a new dynasty, to be culminated by a magnificent building project destined to become a wonder of the ancient world. But unlike the Flavians, this dynasty would be marked by in-fighting, violence, and hatred.

By 193 CE, the Empire was huge, its bureaucracy complicated. Severus couldn't do it all alone. He rounded up the Praetorian Guard, dismissed them all, and replaced them with a trusted corps of his own men. From the outset, his goal was to surround himself with people of unquestionable loyalty. In 198 CE, he appointed his oldest son Caracalla as co-Emperor at the precocious age of ten. In 209 CE, younger son Geta joined the fun as another co-Emperor.

To commemorate the family accomplishments, Severus built a triumphal arch that still stands in the northwest corner of the Forum. Although built to honor Severus, Caracalla, and Geta, one name would eventually be chiseled out, the result of a blood feud.

Despite the power and responsibility thrown at the boys at a young age, it made sense. With conspiracies everywhere, and the Praetorians one missed payment away from murder, sharing the reins of power with family gave Severus an inner circle he could absolutely trust. But not everyone was happy about this. Caracalla seemed to be okay with dad-as-boss, but he really didn't want his bratty younger brother around. The feeling was mutual. Caracalla and Geta despised one another. The only thing that kept the rivalry at bay was their father. And then he died.

On his death bed, Severus would offer one last piece of paternal wisdom, summed up as: "Get along. Honor the troops. Scorn all other men." Severus had understood that the keys to power lie in family unity, a loyal military, and distrust of everyone else. The boys hoped two out of three would suffice.

It didn't take long for their shared antagonism to boil over into downright hatred. Caracalla tried to have Geta assassinated. The plot failed and the rift between the two widened.

Their mother was beside herself. Wasn't the Empire big enough for the two of them? Apparently not. Like children arguing in the back seat of the family car, Caracalla and Geta drew a line. Literally. Geta would have one half of the palace, Caracalla the other. Separate entrances were constructed. Rather than run the Empire, they schemed against each other.

The situation was untenable. One of them had to be the bigger man. As the older brother, Caracalla arranged a peace conference. They would sit down to dinner, just the brothers and their dear mother. Their bodyguards were dismissed. They would talk like adults. They were Emperors; they should act like it.

It was a trap.

While dinner and conversation started, one of Caracalla's soldiers rushed in. Their mom screamed and tried to shield Geta, but the solider butchered the poor young man. Geta died in his mother's arms, hacked to death by his brother's thug, while Caracalla watched with glib satisfaction. The palace was all his now.

Geta was popular; the people were outraged. Caracalla tried to sell self-defense. Playing up the idea of a vast conspiracy, killing squads fanned out across Rome, rounding up anyone associated with—or suspected of being associated with—Geta, and slaughtered them. About 20,000 people died.

The people weren't buying it. Caracalla needed a propaganda coup. He kicked his building program into overdrive. But before he could add, he had to first delete. Caracalla cut his brother's name and image out of the family triumphal arch. Even dead, Geta was being bullied by his older brother. That taken care of, he turned his full architectural attention to a vision so grand that it would come down as one of the wonders of the ancient world.

Down in Alexandria, the public found the self-defense idea laughable. Caracalla didn't like being laughed at. During a visit, he greeted the city elders warmly, invited them to a banquet, and then murdered every last one of them. When rioting broke out, he had the young men of the city rounded up and slaughtered. Twenty-five thousand innocent young people perished in what became known as the "fury of Caracalla." He wasn't exactly "nice." He was more a "genocidal maniac."

Back in the capital, people were starting to get a look at his grand project. What could Caracalla build to make the people forgive his transgressions? A big arena was out. Vespasian had already done that. Aside from bread and circuses, the diversion the Romans enjoyed the most was a trip to the baths. Baths in the Roman world were the hub of social life. People could luxuriate in hot tubs, cool off in a pool, go for a steam, or get a good massage. They could also work out in the gymnasium, listen to a lecture, or strike a business deal. The Romans were class conscious, but in the baths, people of different social strata mixed as nowhere else.

It's not certain if they were begun when Severus was alive. What is certain is that under Caracalla, the building complex that rose was massive. The Baths of Caracalla were built on a scale unlike anything previous.

The complex was about a quarter mile long by a quarter mile wide. The main pool was more than 13,000 square feet. Construction used more than 17 million bricks. There were more than five million cubic feet of basalt used for the foundation. There were hundreds of elegant columns. To feed the oceans of pools, an aqueduct was built to bring in millions of gallons of freshwater. The furnaces for heating tubs, floors, and steam rooms gulped down tons of wood every single day.

To enrich its visitors, the complex was richly adorned with mosaics and sculpture. Visitors could look after their spiritual heath by paying their respects to the god Mithras in his sanctuary. Libraries with extensive collections were assembled for scholars. The finest frescoes graced its ceilings and walls. The whole complex was swathed in luxurious gardens for quiet meditation. The baths were the height of artistic style, culture, and good taste. To top it all off, they were open to the public, and you couldn't beat the price: free. Caracalla wanted the people to like him. Or at least stop hating him.

But karma, or justice, caught up with Caracalla in 217 CE while traveling. Even the undisputed master of Rome had to obey when nature called. Taking advantage of his vulnerable state, a disgruntled soldier stabbed Caracalla by the side of a road. Not to get too far ahead of ourselves, but in case you are wondering, the death of Caracalla did not usher in a new era of peace and stability.

Back in Rome, Caracalla was not deeply mourned. Maybe the Romans couldn't be bought off that easily. Or maybe all the bathers were just too relaxed to care much.

Even in its ruined state, it's easy to be overwhelmed by the massive scale of the Baths of Caracalla. When you consider the man behind the project, it makes a visitor pause. Grand though they may have been—truly a wonder of its age—the nature of their builder sends chills up the spine. Caracalla was a vicious man who thought nothing of using his power to kill and murder.

Tour the baths. Admire the scope and grandeur of the complex. Find the remains of the intricate mosaic floors; imagine the sunlight shimmering on the pools; marvel at what it took to make it all work. Appreciate the artistry, the engineering. Contemplate what it would have been like to enjoy the facilities, exercising mind and body, letting go of the stress of every day.

Above all, consider who Caracalla was and what he stood for. Remember his poor mother, holding the dying Geta, murdered by his own brother, her other son. Remember the slaughter of Geta's supporters, and of the liquidation of Alexandrian youth, the tens of thousands of lives extinguished. All of the bathing, steaming, and scrubbing couldn't wash away the blood of such unspeakable acts.

➤ How to get to the Baths of Caracalla

The Baths of Caracalla are on the south side of Rome. They are hard to miss, as the imposing ruins have little around to compete for your attention. They are a ten-minute walk from the Circo Massimo Metro Station (Line B), and a twenty-minute walk from the Colosseum.

Address: Viale delle Terme di Caracalla, 52.

Phone number: +39 06 3996 7700

➤ Hours

The hours of the Baths vary, but they are generally open by 9:00 a.m. and close between 5:00 p.m. and 7:00 p.m.

Check the following website for more specific times: *www .turismoroma.it/cosa-fare/terme-di-caracalla?lang=en*.

➤ Local eats

Sample another ancient culture's cuisine at a small, Greek-run diner:

Elleniko ($)
Viale Aventino 109, 00153
+39 06 6442 0648
www.facebook.com/ellenikoroma

Dine day-round, with breakfast, brunch, lunch, or dinner:

Max Roma ($$)
Viale Aventino 20, 00153
+39 06 6442 0669
www.maxroma.it/

Look for celebrities in a celebrated trattoria dating back to 1936 (reservations required):

Felice a Testaccio ($$)
Roma Via Mastro Giorgio 29, 00153
+39 06 574 6800
www.feliceatestaccio.it/

Savor a slice at one of the top pizzerias in Rome:
Sbanco ($$)
Via Siria, 1, 00183
+39 06 789318
www.facebook.com/Sbanco-440376599420200/

➤ Want more of the story before the next chapter? *You'll have to Mind the Gap.*

Wander around Rome long enough and you may notice something odd. The more you look for it, the more you see it, or, more precisely, don't see it. For all the temples, palaces, arenas, and arches, there are gaps. From the time of the founding of Rome, and for 1,000 years thereafter, each era in the city's long and winding history is well-represented in the archaeological record. But when you look at the date of various buildings, there is a large chunk of time in the 3rd century CE where nothing seems to have been built.

How could this be? With monumental architecture such an important part of Roman society, how could nearly a century pass without much being added?

For Emperors, monumental building was critical to conveying imperial legitimacy. A quick scan of the history

of Rome in the fifty-year span from 235 to 285 CE indi-
cates legitimacy was on short order. Emperors rose and
fell so quickly that they never really had time to under-
take big-picture projects. In one fun year, 238 CE, there
were no fewer than six claimants to the throne. Valuing
accuracy more than imagination, historians call this the
Year of Six Emperors. Nothing typified the struggles
Rome was facing more than this undignified chaos.

With reigns measured in months, or even days, it's
no wonder Emperors couldn't plan long-term projects.
Granted, few of them knew in advance their rules would
be so short, but when each rose as part of some dramatic
upheaval, dealing with the immediate aftershocks seems
to have absorbed their entire attention. Then the cycle
began anew with a new claimant, a new reaction, more
violence, and war.

The best some could manage was not to build, but to
renovate. During this chaotic time, the Colosseum got
some needed work. The Baths of Titus got a makeover,
as did the Baths of Trajan. The best that most of the
short-lived rulers could manage was to try and patch up
older structures, to glom on to the glory of the original.

The Emperor Decius managed to commission a new
set of baths on the Aventine Hill, but it's questionable if
he lived long enough to see their completion. Either way,

only tiny fragments remain and, like the Emperor himself, they are nearly forgotten.

As you wander around Rome, take careful note of the dates of buildings and monuments; notice the telling gap in the record. The glory days were gone. Better times were ahead. But for this period . . . chaos.

Today, an old wall might show up in a basement. Some stones here and there may date to the period. But by and large, there was not a lot of new building going on for most of the 3rd century. Rome was beset by catastrophic political infighting and disastrous military defeats. For people living in that fifty-year period, power, glory, and stability had been replaced by fear, acrimony, and betrayal.

CHAPTER 10

The Walls of Aurelian

There are a lot of ways to get into Rome. Those flying into Leonardo da Vinci International Airport take a train into the city, as do visitors from other Italian cities. Modern roads give drivers many points of access. Pedestrians can simply walk there. It wasn't always so easy to get into the city. In fact, at one point, the Romans were more interested in keeping people out.

In the mid-3rd century CE, the Empire was teetering on the verge of collapse. Despite all of its pressing challenges, the city had to be protected from enemies and marauding barbarians. Just when all seemed as though it might be lost, two things happened: a series of brilliant Emperors led a dramatic reversal of fortune, and the capital was secured with the completion of the Walls of Aurelian, which added a level of security Rome hadn't known—or needed—in centuries.

Even for historians, some 3rd-century rulers are obscure, shrouded in unknowns and uncertainty. It was a terrible time to have the top job. But the lure of unconditional power was too much of a siren song, and one after another, Emperors grabbed the throne only to be usurped, pushed aside, or murdered. Between the death of the last of the Severan family and the rise of Aurelian, life expectancy upon becoming Emperor was less than three years.

In that span, there were fifteen Emperors. Half didn't make it to a year. Some ruled for mere days. All but two Emperors in this period died a violent death, at the hands of assassins, in battle, or by suicide. Before we feel any measure of comfort for the two exceptions, they both appear to have died of plague. By way of contrast, consider that the Julio-Claudians, even with Caligula's short reign, managed an average term of nearly nineteen years.

Being Emperor was a messy, deadly business. Still, there was no shortage of people who wanted the job. The real shortage was people who could actually do the job, at least with any measure of competency. These were troubled times. It's no wonder that they're called the Crisis of the Third Century.

The Walls of Aurelian.

The constant in-fighting and power grabs sapped the Empire's strength when it needed it most. Out in the provinces and on their borders, native tribes grew in population, strength, and a sense of their own sovereignty. Huge swaths of the Empire calved like icebergs, and the constant power struggles back in Rome undermined any Emperor's ability to do anything about it.

Emperors and armies were in a constant state of reaction, responding to this emergency or that. For the first time in a long time, the safety of Rome itself was in doubt. The power of the Empire had been reduced so much that it wasn't inconceivable that a foreign army could come crashing down the Italian peninsula and threaten the capital.

Amidst all this, the power of the Empire had shifted east. As time marched relentlessly on, Rome's position was increasingly symbolic and less a reflection of its true center of military and political strength. The city of Rome was not what it used to be. But, even if just a symbol, it was an extremely powerful one. Rome was the ceremonial heart of the Empire, from where its greatest leaders hailed, where their ancestors were buried, where their marble monuments still glistened in the bright sun. It had to be protected.

Things really had begun to fall apart. In the west, a renegade general had decided he could set up his own Empire and revolted against the mothership. His name was Postumus and he judged that Rome could no longer protect the provinces. He thought he could do better. In 260 CE he rebelled, murdered the son of the Emperor, and put together a kingdom that was massive in its own right, encompassing part or all of modern-day Britain, Spain, France, and Germany. He modeled his Gallic Empire on the institutions of Rome, with annually-elected consuls and a Senate. In 268 CE, Postumus was murdered by his own troops, angered because he had refused to let them sack an enemy city. His kingdom was inherited by less vigorous rulers, but it remained a thorn in the side of the Roman Empire.

In the east, the wily queen Zenobia had sensed her opportunity. Ruler of the client kingdom Palmyra, Zenobia had smelled blood in the water and revolted in 270 CE, overthrowing Roman control and forging her own empire, which covered much of the modern Middle East and Egypt. Losing Roman territory to a Roman renegade was one thing. Having the Empire's territory taken by a foreigner—a *queen* no less—was another thing entirely.

To top it all off, marauding bands of Germanic tribes called Goths were causing trouble all over the place. The Romans couldn't address the bigger issue of its fracturing Empire without leaving itself vulnerable to their attack. Should they march off to confront either breakaway kingdom, the door to Rome would be left wide open. It seemed that the Roman Empire was drawing to a close.

Then some people started to know what they were doing. More and more, it wasn't Roman nobles from ancient families that could do the job; it was vigorous generals from across the Adriatic Sea. Some of Rome's most effective and dynamic Emperors weren't from Rome, but rather the far-off province of Illyria. It was these generals that would slow, and then halt the course of Roman decline, eventually stitching the Empire back together and stewarding it through the Crisis of the Third Century.

The tide began to turn with the rise of Claudius Gothicus as Emperor in 268 CE. In his short reign, the capable general won a series of wars with Germanic tribes, stemming their rise and freeing the Empire up to focus on other existential threats. Unfortunately, Claudius caught the plague and died a year and a half after his ascension. His successor lasted about a month, barely enough to leave a mark. Fortunately, the next guy in line would leave a bigger legacy.

Aurelian had shot up through the ranks under Claudius, eventually becoming the number-two man behind the Emperor. He was a capable administrator and an effective general. Upon claiming the throne, he faced an immediate crisis: barbarian tribes had invaded Italy. For the first time in a long time, the capital was in crisis, under threat from foreign enemies. Aurelian defeated the invaders in a series of running battles. While everyone breathed a sigh of relief, the lesson was not lost on Aurelian. The city was vulnerable. Aurelian drew up plans for a massive circuit of walls and defensive fortifications to protect the people, their buildings, and their way of life.

In 271 CE, construction began in earnest. Rome hadn't upgraded its defensive walls since the 4th century BCE (you can still see a portion of the Servian Wall outside Termini station), and the city had long since outgrown them. What the engineers accomplished was nothing short of spectacular.

The Aurelian Walls, built between 271 and 275 CE, enclosed nearly five and a half square miles within a wall that was more than ten feet thick, nearly thirty feet high, and punctuated by a defensive tower every one hundred feet. To save time and money, the walls incorporated existing buildings as much as possible, such as the Pyramid of Cestius. The completion of the walls in such a short period of time was a triumph of engineering and brought great relief to the people.

Aurelian, always on to the next challenge, did not stay in the city to supervise construction. With the barbarian threat settled, Aurelian set his sights on the bigger picture. He deemed the province of Dacia to be indefensible, and withdrew Roman troops back across the Danube River. In the process, he ordered the demolition of Apollodorus's magnificent bridge.

With more secure borders, he turned his attention to the east, leading his army to confront queen Zenobia of the breakaway Palmyrene Empire. The Palmyrenes had taken much of Rome's eastern empire, including Egypt. In a time when famine was a frequent threat, Rome couldn't afford to let Egypt's agricultural production slip away. In 272–273 CE, the talented Aurelian made quick work of Zenobia, and brought the lands of the east back under Roman sway. They tried to revolt again, and a furious Aurelian had the rebel leaders executed.

Aurelian was off to a good start. He had defended the motherland, bested marauding tribes, and begun construction of a huge upgrade to Rome's defenses. But he wasn't done yet. Shortly after defeating Zenobia, Aurelian turned to the breakaway Gallic Empire. Making haste for the west, Aurelian defeated its ineffectual leaders, successfully completing his reunification of the entire Empire. He was acknowledged as "Restitutor Orbis," or, "Restorer of the World." Aurelian was even hailed as "Master and God." Rome wasn't free and clear of the Crisis of the Third Century, but thanks to an Emperor who didn't have to wait to die to be deified, the worst was past.

Unfortunately for Aurelian, and all of Rome, not even such an exalted leader was safe from plots. A low-ranking official in Aurelian's administration had committed some transgression. Afraid of the Emperor's retribution, the official forged a document, which he claimed was Aurelian's list of officials to be executed for treason. The official showed the fake document to the condemned, many of whom were in Aurelian's inner circle. Taking the document at face value, they struck Aurelian before he could act against them. The death of Aurelian came just as Rome was getting on solid footing and was a completely unnecessary tragedy for the Empire. One can only imagine what Aurelian would have been able to accomplish with a full term in office. It is one of history's greatest "what ifs."

He did not live to see the completion of the walls that today bear his name, which were completed shortly after his death. Today, you can visit the walls in many different places across the city. Parts have been demolished to make way for modern infrastructure. Other sections were torn down in the medieval period; others have simply fallen into ruin. Yet, large sections of the walls remain; about two thirds of the original.

They are all over Rome, here and there. There are many different places to see them; chances are you may already have. If you haven't come across the walls yet, then consider making the trip down to the Porta San Sebastiano. It is the largest preserved gate through the Aurelian Walls, and it is flanked by a large section of intact wall. The gate plays host to lots of graffiti, carved into the brick and travertine through the centuries. A close inspection reveals an elaborate carving of a stoic Archangel Michael slaying a dragon, accompanied by an inscription in Medieval Latin.

Perhaps the best reason to make this your spot to view the Walls of Aurelian is that within Porta San Sebastiano is the Museum of the Walls, which affords visitors—free of charge—the chance to walk in and around the gatehouse, and along a well-preserved section of the walls.

Through the vigor of a series of competent and energetic rules, the Roman Empire managed to live on for another 200 years. Thank goodness it did, because some of the most interesting places and people are yet to come. The walls are a focal point in the reestablishment of the integrated Roman Empire, but also a symbol of the shift of Rome itself from center of world domination to ceremonial symbol of the past. Enter the gatehouse and explore the museum. Walk outside on the walls. Climb to the top of the tower and look down the Appian Way, history's most famous road. Remember why the walls were built and what was happening inside the troubled Empire at the time. Imagine what it was like to be a soldier patrolling the walls, staying ever-vigilant to threats, both foreign and domestic. For the first time in hundreds of years, people who never had to consider foreign threats were faced with increasing uncertainty and vulnerability. Although the walls could help add a measure of comfort, knowing that they were needed in the first place was a poignant reminder of just how far Rome had fallen.

➤ How to get to the Walls of Aurelian

The walls are all over the city. You may have already come across them. If you go to the Museum of the Walls, then this is the furthest out-of-the-way point in this book. It's worth it. Located in the southeast of the city, the museum is about a half hour walk from both the Ponte Lungo Metro Station (Line A) and the Colosseum.

Address: Via di Porta San Sebastiano, 18, 00179 Roma.

Phone Number: +39 060608

Website: *http://en.museodellemuraroma.it/*

Hours: Daily, from 9:00 a.m. to 2:00 p.m.

➤ Travel tip

The museum abuts the Park of the Scipioni, named for one of the most prominent patrician families of the Roman Republic. It contains their family tomb, which is worth the trip in its own right.

➤ Local eats

Cheer a soccer/football team in a family-friendly restaurant with large portions:

    Core de Roma ($)
    Via Vetulonia 27, 00153
    +39 06 700 0475
    https://corederoma27.wordpress.com/

Get your sushi fix:

Hari Ristorante Giapponese ($$)

Via Acaia 39, 00183

+39 06 7720 4177

www.harirestaurant.com/

Enjoy your meal in great outdoor garden seating:

Ristorante Da Orazio a Caracalla ($$)

Via di Porta Latina 5, 00179

+39 06 7049 2401

www.ristoranteorazio.it/

Try something new by visiting this authentic Peruvian restaurant:

Imperio Inca I ($$)

Largo Pannonia 17/18, 00183

+39 06 8901 6955

www.ristoranteimperioinca1.it/

➤ Want more of the story before the next chapter? *Stop by the Baths of Diocletian.*

Much of Rome's history is about conflict: between ambitious politicians, between rival generals, between Rome and its foreign enemies. Those who emerged victorious carved the stories of their victory in stone all around the

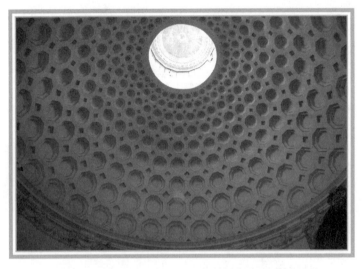

San Bernardo alla Terme, one of the churches built from/in the ruins of the Baths of Diocletian.

city. As the Roman Empire sought to regain its footing from the Crisis of the Third Century, Emperors began to build again. In 298 CE, construction began on the Baths of Diocletian, the largest imperial baths ever constructed, to demonstrate that the perpetual conflict of the previous generations was over. But these baths are a reminder that the most consequential conflict was not in the temporal world, but the spiritual one.

As early as the reign of Nero, Christians became the target of imperial ire. Nero came under suspicion of ordering the Great Fire set himself. To deflect these accusations, he cast blame on and executed several Christians.

During the short-lived reign of Decius, an edict was passed that all Romans must sacrifice to the gods and to the well-being of the Emperor. For anyone other than Roman pagans, this forced a choice between compromising one's religious beliefs—and thus imperiling their spiritual well-being—or death.

The most vigorous persecution of Christians came under Diocletian, who issued proclamations stripping Christians of citizenship and demanding, under pain of death, their conversion to the traditional Roman religion.

It's easy to look back on these Emperors with a jaundiced glare. History judges their actions scornfully. But it is important to ask: Why did they do it in the first place?

Emperors projected themselves as semi-divine; having "one true god" as competition challenged imperial legitimacy. Christian persecutions were less about theology, and more about continuity and unquestioned obedience to the Emperor. Diocletian reigned in a time of instability. Restoration of Rome to the top of the world order meant reconnecting with the traditions that built the Empire. The gods had served Rome well for more than 1,000 years; why turn away now? Religious persecutions weren't driven by megalomania. That was little consolation to victims though.

History would afford the Christians the last laugh. The baths of the most vigorous persecutor have yielded not one but two Christian churches. Michelangelo himself was commissioned to create the Basilica of St. Mary of the Angels and the Martyrs from the ruins. Another church, San Bernardo alle Terme, recycled other sections of the complex. One can only imagine how Diocletian would feel to know that a grand building in his name has yielded safe places of worship for those whom he once persecuted.

Stand outside the Basilica and face the concave entrance; it's as though the church is trying to draw you closer. Off to the right, the façade ends abruptly at the rough edges of a shattered wall, reminding visitors of the building's great age and complicated history. To the left, the Basilica adjoins a more modern structure, leaning on its neighbor for support. The most important thing to see before stepping inside is the cross above the entrance. It's a reminder that the legacy of Roman conflict was carved not only in stone, but also in the soul.

Address: Piazza della Repubblica.

Nearest Metro: Republica, Metro Line A (seven-minute walk), a fifteen-minute walk from the Colosseum.

Tip: Basilica of St. Mary of the Angels and the Martyrs is open daily from 7:00 a.m. to 6:30 p.m. (7:30 p.m. on Sundays). While you are in the area, be sure to visit San Bernardo alle Terme, as well as the branch of the National Roman Museum, both also built in the ruins of the Baths of Diocletian.

CHAPTER 11

Scala Santa

For many of the millions of visitors that come to Rome each year, the true wonder is to walk in the footsteps of legendary people who shaped history. A stroll down the Via Sacra is to join Caesar in his Triumphs. To climb the steps to the altar of the Ara Pacis is to sacrifice with Augustus. To amble through the Pantheon is to join Hadrian in admiration of its architectural perfection. But in one very special place, the opportunity is not to walk, but to kneel in reverence.

It's not unusual for Roman temples and churches to be fronted by a staircase, as though a visitor is ascending to a higher, holier plane. What is unusual about the stairs at the front of the Church of St. Lawrence in Palatio is not what they are made of or where they are located, it's who climbed them: Jesus. As in *the* Jesus. But how could

The Holy Stairs, the Scala Santa, upon which Jesus walked on his way to and from his fateful meeting with Pilate.

a set of stairs in from Jerusalem dating from the time of Jesus end up in a Renaissance-era church in Rome?

When Diocletian rose to power in 284 CE, he knew the job was too much for one guy to handle alone. In an unusual move, he realized that the solution was to share power. Within a couple of years, he appointed a co-Emperor, Maximian. Diocletian would primarily rule the east, Maximian the west. But the Empire was huge, and a simple split wouldn't solve the issue. Besides, Diocletian knew they wouldn't be around forever. He also wanted to solve the issue of succession, making sure they could be replaced by competent, experienced administrators.

Accordingly, he appointed two junior Emperors to join the fun. When the appointed time came, Diocletian and Maximian would retire and be replaced by their subordinates, Constantius and Galerius. They, in turn, would each appoint a new junior Emperor. This rotation of power was to take place every ten years. A constant stream of good and experienced people would provide a solid foundation, and access to office would eliminate in-fighting and civil war.

It was a brilliant administrative solution to the chronic issues of the Empire. There was just one problem: It flew in the face of human nature. There were some very ambitious people, most notably, the sons of

Constantius and Maximian, who didn't want to wait their turn, and it wouldn't take long for the whole system to fall apart.

Just a year after taking over as the senior Emperor, Constantius grew ill and died. His son Constantine ignored the carefully prepared transition plan and cut to the front of the line. Back in Rome, Maximian's son Maxentius was miffed about being left out of the plans too. He rebelled, seized Rome, and declared himself Emperor. The actions of the two precocious would-be Emperors set off a complicated series of events that at one point even included Maximian deciding that retirement wasn't for him, and trying to reclaim the throne for himself. It was all a big, confusing mess, with rebellions, counter-rebellions, and shifting allegiances. At one point, someone suggested to Diocletian that he come out of retirement to get things straightened out. He declined. The reason he stated: He was really happy growing cabbages at his palace. All things considered, it was a smart move.

Those who remained in the power struggle continued to slug it out. By the time the dust settled, there were two remaining claimants to the western throne, and neither wanted to share with the other. In control of Rome was Maxentius, and marching on the capital was

The faithful in prayer on the Scala Santa.

Constantine. In 312 CE, the two armies, about 200,000 soldiers combined, sized each other up, ready to battle for control of the western Empire. But what looked like another battle in another civil war would turn out to be much more, forever altering the course of human history.

On the night before the fateful day, Constantine had a vision in which the Christian God told him to paint the first two letters of Christ's name in Greek on the shields of his soldiers. God, Constantine had claimed, would offer his protection in return. The shields were duly painted and the next day, Constantine routed Maxentius, who drowned in the Tiber trying to flee. Constantine entered Rome in triumph. In his mind, the Christian God was more powerful than the entire pagan pantheon put together. Two trends were irreversible: Constantine was on his way to having "The Great," attached to his name, and Christianity was on its way to becoming the official religion of the Roman Empire.

At first, the two halves of the Empire were cooperative. The eastern Emperor was Constantine's brother-in-law. The two oversaw the Edict of Milan, a groundbreaking proclamation that officially granted toleration of Christianity. The days of persecution were (almost) a thing of the past. But why content yourself with half the Empire, when having the whole thing would be so much more fun? In due time, Constantine picked and won a fight with his sister's husband. Rome was back to one Emperor. The brilliant administrative reforms of Diocletian barely outlived him.

In a way, it is fitting: The first monotheistic Emperor was the sole ruler over the entire Empire. But even the everywhere-at-once Constantine knew that the focal point of Roman power had shifted east. For a man who saw himself as a new kind of Emperor, a city steeped in the past was less interesting than one with an unlimited future. After careful scouting, Constantine selected a site for a new imperial capital at the ancient city of Byzantium. His engineers and architects planned and built a city that the preening Emperor duly christened "New Rome." The name wasn't terribly catchy, and in short order, everyone just called it "Constantinople," after its eponymous founder.

But monumental building and sole control of the Empire wasn't quite enough for Constantine. In order to demonstrate divine favor, he needed a more tangible connection to God. Constantine was a busy man and needed a partner to help him accomplish his ambitious goals. He turned to the person he trusted above all others: his mother. The Empress Helena was dispatched to the Holy Land with an imperial retinue and a mission to collect relics from the life and times of Jesus. With a physical connection to the son of God, Constantine could lay claim to a special relationship with the big guy, elevating his status above all other mortal men.

Helena set off for Jerusalem at the tender age of eighty. When she arrived, she found a city still trying to heal from the tumult of Titus's sacking nearly 300 years earlier, and further damage wrought by Hadrian's vindictive Jewish persecutions. In addition to artifact hunting, Helena sought to heal the emotional breach between the Empire and its most holy city. Her trip was a smashing success. She commissioned the building of churches at the sites of Jesus's birth and ascension to heaven. She claimed discovery of the tomb of Jesus, pieces of the True Cross, and thorns from the crown of thorns. Some of the discoveries were a little weird, like the finger Doubting Thomas used to probe the wounds of Jesus.

One fascinating relic the octogenarian Helena came across was the staircase leading to the office of Pontius Pilate, the Roman governor who had adjudicated the trial of Jesus. It was over these steps that Jesus walked on his way to and from his fateful meeting with Pilate. For the faithful back in Rome, it was a poignant reminder of the Empire's role in the death of the founder of the new faith that was winning so many adherents. The staircase created lots of opportunities for contemplation and reflection, and could bring people in literal contact with the footsteps of Jesus. Powerful indeed, the stairs were crated up and added to Helena's treasure trove.

Perhaps it was from exhaustion from the arduous journey, or perhaps it was simply that she was nearly twenty years past the average life expectancy for the time, but Helena died around the same time the goods landed in Rome. Today, she is considered a saint in many Christian religions. Many of the relics she discovered survive to this day.

Constantine didn't inherit his mom's longevity genes. He grew ill and infirm at age sixty-five. Wanting to make sure that he entered heaven with a clean slate, he is purported to only have converted to the religion he did so much to advance on his death bed. The legacy of Constantine the Great is complex and his story is fascinating, the subject of much interpretation. What's undebatable is the profound impact that he had in creating the modern world. Well, with a little help from his mom, that is. Any visitor to Rome can experience the legacy they left behind, and get up close and personal with another guy who had a pretty big hand in shaping the world as we know it.

Today, the area of the Lateran, a short walk southeast from the Colosseum, is chock-full of great places to visit and cool things to see. The obelisk in the square is from the reign of Tuthmose III, one of the greatest pharaohs in Egypt's long history. The showpiece is the Archbasilica of San Giovanni in Laterano. The church is the seat of the Bishop of Rome, more commonly called the Pope. It is considered to be the mother church of the Catholic faith, and it is adorned with elaborate decorations and symbols of God's divine favor. It was constructed by none other than Constantine himself. It is a public place; the spectacle and pomp of Catholic ceremony and the crowds around it prove its importance.

But when the Popes wanted a quiet place to pray, they sought somewhere else to go. They could retire to their palace to escape the populace. Through the centuries, the papal palace fell into disrepair. Parts of it were knocked down to make room for a new building. This renovation unveiled one of the secrets contained within. The Scala Santa, or sacred staircase, had been embedded within the old palace. Once contained within the private sanctuary of Popes and Emperors, the Scala Santa were relocated across from San Giovanni to the entrance to the church of St. Lawrence in Palatio, and are now available to anyone, of any faith or creed. The only thing that is asked is a respect for tradition.

Enter into the building. It's not hard to know what to do; many people will show the way. These days, the stairs, which are encased in wood for protection, are not for feet; they are for knees. Those who wish may kneel, and say a prayer on each of the twenty-eight steps. You can join the contemplative experience of being so close to arguably the most transcendent figure in history. Let your knees find the well-worn grooves formed by the millions of people that have come before you. It's a physically demanding experience, but it can be quite moving.

If prayer is not your thing, no worries. The Scala Santa is flanked by ordinary staircases that climb to the top of the landing. Regardless of faith or creed, it's almost surreal to contemplate following the footsteps of Jesus on his way to judgment at the hands of Pontius Pilate. All it took for Constantine to follow the literal footsteps of the father of one of the world's great religions was a little help from his mom.

➤ How to get to Scala Santa

The Scala Santa is located in the section of the city called the Lateran, on the southeast side of the city. It is a ten-minute walk from the San Giovanni Metro Station (Line A) and a twenty-minute walk from the Colosseum.

Address: Piazza di S. Giovanni in Laterano, 14.

Phone number: +39 06 7726641

➤ Hours

Daily from 6:30 a.m. to 6:30 p.m.; on Sundays and during summer, the opening time is 7:00 a.m. During summer, the closing time is 7:00 p.m. It is occasionally closed for periods in mid-day.

➤ Travel tip

At the top of the staircase is another revered artifact: an icon that, according to legend, was begun by none other than Saint Luke the Evangelist, author of the Gospel of Luke and the Acts of the Apostles. The icon is one of the "Acheiropoieta," meaning, made without hands. According to tradition, though Luke began the icon, it was finished by an angel. Through the centuries, it has been embellished, restored, and covered over many times, so it is impossible to get a glimpse of what it looked like when first created.

➤ Local eats

Grab a sandwich or quick bite:
Bred Bottega Gourmet ($)
Piazza di San Giovanni in Laterano 46, Zona San Giovanni, 00184
+39 06 8769 1514

Enjoy a classic Italian meal in a nice setting:
Trattoria Vecchia Roma ($$)
Via Ferruccio, 12B/C, 00185
+39 06 44 67 143
www.trattoriavecchiaroma.it

Take in a casual, traditional Roman restaurant:
I Buoni Amici ($$)
Via Aleardo Aleardi 4, 00185
+39 06 7049 1993

Have a dining adventure where the menu changes every week (reservations recommended):
Machiavelli's Club ($$)
Via Machiavelli 49, 00185
+39 347 454 0179
www.clubmachiavelli.it/

➤ Want more of the story before the next chapter? *Stop by Santa Croce in Gerusalemme.*

Some churches in Rome you find simply by walking down the street. Others are a bit out of the way; you need to be looking for them. Santa Croce in Gerusalemme is worth the extra steps off the beaten path, not only for what awaits inside, but for what the church itself represents.

You can admire the baroque façade, but don't be fooled by the exterior; stepping inside brings us back 1,700 years into the world of Constantine and Helena, always an interesting place to be.

Helena was of humble background, offering little in the way of political connections and resources. Accordingly, Constantius divorced her when a new bride of higher stature became available. She was sent away, and their son, the future Emperor Constantine was sent to the other side of the Empire to the court of Diocletian. Constantine learned his lessons well.

Helena was a devout woman, whose piety influenced her ambitious son. He, in turn, was dedicated to her. After all the tumult that brought about Constantine's rise, one of his first acts was to send for Helena and cloak her in honors befitting the mother of the Emperor, including installing her in a new palace. The pious

Helena converted a room in her new digs into a chapel for private family Christian worship. When she returned from her trip to the Holy Land, this chapel housed many of the relics.

One of the unusual things she brought back was a big pile of dirt. Helena had the floor of her chapel covered with the soil from the Holy Land, so that even in Rome she and her family could be connected to the sacred with every step. The church that rose out from and around Helena's chapel is not "in Jerusalem"; rather, Jerusalem is in it.

Helena's chapel and the church that grew from it offer more than a connection to the Constantinians and the early days of Christianity. Santa Croce in Gerusalemme is a symbol of the end of one epoch and the beginning of another. Before the rise of Constantine, Christianity swung between being discretely tolerated and viciously persecuted. From that point forward, monumental building in Rome changed. No more theatres, no more forums, and, most importantly, no more temples. More than a millennium of architectural heritage drew to a close. As Christianity took over the Empire, the rulers of Rome narrowed their building efforts to churches.

Certainly, Christian worship had begun in the city long before. But prior to its official legitimization by

Constantine, early Christians did so in secret. With the faith of Helena, and the eventual conversion of Constantine, Christianity came out of the shadows and took center stage.

Step into Santa Croce in Gerusalemme; work your way to the room housing the holy relics. You are at the origin of the transformation of Rome from a city of temples to a city of churches. The dirt has vanished, but the idea of a Roman connection to the Holy Land lives on. Helena's humble family chapel grew, not only into the larger basilica you find today, but into an idea: Christianity was the official religion of the Empire and Rome was the spiritual heart of the world.

Address: Piazza di Santa Croce in Gerusalemme, 12.

Nearest Metro: Lodi, Metro Line C (ten-minute walk), a thirty-minute walk from the Colosseum.

Tip: Visit *www.santacroceroma.it/en/* for more information.

CHAPTER 12

The Column of Phocas

A new Emperor seized power in Constantinople with visions of restoring the Roman Emperor to its former glory, completing the reunification of east and west, and proclaiming himself as the sovereign of the renewed Empire. To mark his eternal glory, and remind the people in the old capital of the dawning of the new era, the eastern Emperor Phocas celebrated as a new triumphal column rose in the Forum in his honor.

The Column of Phocas is a little piecemeal; the various components are mismatched. The base once propped up a statue of Diocletian. The column itself was taken from an older building. No matter. The designer was less interested in architectural harmony than in the message it conveyed: There was a new Emperor in Constantinople, and the Romans were supportive. The part of the monument Phocas would want people to notice was the magnificent gold statue of himself at its top.

But rather than a portent of a new beginning, it heralded the end. The Column of Phocas was destined to be the last addition to the Roman Forum, bringing to close a tradition of monumental building that had lasted almost a millennium and a half.

As Roman power in the west waned then collapsed, the power of the Empire shifted to the east, with Constantinople as the base of operations for a new crop of energetic, ambitious rulers. The long, steady decline of the western Roman Empire reached its climax in 476 CE, when the last western Emperor was deposed, replaced by a strongman who styled himself as king. The poor sixteen-year-old boy whom history records as the last western Emperor was sent into exile to live out his days in obscurity. He carried a fitting name for the last Emperor, Romulus Augustulus. It seems only appropriate that the last western Emperor paid homage to both the founder, and to the first Emperor of mighty Rome.

By the time of Romulus's deposition, Roman power had contracted to a hollow shell of its former self. The city had long since ceased to be the capital. Emperors in the west had first moved their operations to Milan, then

The Column of Phocas.

Ravenna. Although its political power had been almost completely extinguished, the city of Rome's symbolic position as the center of Roman identity lived on, if only in memory. Even after little Romulus was pushed aside, and a pretender occupied the throne room in Ravenna, Rome was still in the hearts and minds of many.

Something as momentous as the collapse of the western Empire deserved a spectacular send-off. But it was decidedly understated, more like a faint candle flickering out than a flash of lightning or explosion of fireworks. Modern readers have the benefit of seeing the arc of history all at once, but living through events can offer a very different perspective. The line between Empire and collapse was not so clearly drawn in the minds of the people living through events as they happened.

But many, including the Emperors in the eastern Empire, knew that a fundamental shift had occurred. Their reach was diminished; the sovereignty of Constantinople challenged. For more than a century after the collapse of the western Empire, the rulers in the east struggled to assert their dominion and keep the whole thing together. Sometimes they succeeded. Often, they did not. In fits and starts, various rulers in Constantinople claimed authority over the west, and of the old capital, once the beating heart of the

Empire. They launched campaigns. Armies marched. Navies sailed. Commanders battled, sometimes winning, sometimes losing. Long after the reality of the united Empire was extinguished, the flame of memory burned on. The eastern Emperors imagined the personal glory to be had for the man who finally brought it all back together.

The closest anyone came was the Emperor Justinian, who ruled from 527 to 565 CE. Under the generalship of his brilliant commander Belisarius, Justinian saw considerable success in the quest to restore the united Empire. But just as things were getting good, a horrific plague broke out, devastating Constantinople and sapping the strength of its armies. The traditional borders of the Empire melted away. He had won a good deal of Italy back, but the territorial holdings were far from contiguous, with blotches here and there, more Rorschach inkblots than an even coat of paint. A governor appointed by Constantinople ruled this piecemeal assortment of lands from Ravenna; one city that was in the eastern Empire's holdings was Rome.

Justinian's successor was crazy. Literally. Aware that he was losing his grasp on reality, he chose an heir before he completely lost his marbles. This ruler, Justin II, ruled for a few short years before turning things over to

Maurice. By all accounts, Maurice did a good job and he had a long reign. But after a while, one of his generals decided he could do better, and began scheming.

Phocas was a senior general under Maurice. He declared a rebellion, took his army, marched on Constantinople and deposed the sitting Emperor. Maurice was a spent force. But rather than let him live out his days in harmless obscurity, Phocas flashed a cruel streak. He dragged the poor ex-Emperor out of prison, made him watch each of his six sons be butchered, then finished off the bereft old man. The real bummer for the gang in Constantinople was that Maurice was a good Emperor. He had vanquished foes and restored dignity to Constantinople. Phocas was more interested in naked power than good policy.

Maybe it was with his cruelty in mind that the folks back in Rome wanted to erect a monument to show Phocas what a swell guy they thought he was. Better to kiss up to an unscrupulous ne'er-do-well than to pick a fight with him. Or perhaps the governor, who had been thrown out of office because of his own apparent insanity, was just really grateful when Phocas gave him his old job back. He wouldn't last long, but Phocas did have one act that had a more lasting impact on the Eternal City; he donated the Pantheon to the Pope for its conversion to a church. Given the Church's mania for ripping down anything they considered pagan, Phocas's gift might just have saved the magnificent building for posterity.

When the column in his honor was erected, Phocas imagined a new dawn for the Roman world, a restoration of how things had been, honoring the long history of a united and powerful empire. But this was a delusion. By the time it was erected, the Column of Phocas was already obsolete, not in terms of building materials or architectural style, but in terms of what it meant and represented.

The idea of a unified Roman Empire was gone forever. With it was the idea of benevolent Emperors, adorning the Eternal City with monuments, public buildings, and places of worship. A few hundred years later would see a schismatic split between Rome and Constantinople, with the Eastern Orthodox Church going its own way; Rome's claim as the spiritual capital of all of Christendom was likewise marginalized. The fracture that divided east and west was never to be healed. The Column of Phocas is less a symbol of the eternal glory of its namesake, than it is a poignant endpoint, reminding all just how far Rome had fallen. Phocas barely outlived the completion of the monument.

In the east, the Roman Emperors would rule from Constantinople until the city fell to the Turks in 1453 CE, nearly 1,000 years later. Historians call the eastern Empire "Byzantine," to mark the fracturing of empire and the shift of power to Constantinople. The term would have been meaningless in its time. It's just a device used by historians. They considered themselves to be Roman.

From the time that Rome was founded in 753 BCE, to the time of Constantinople's collapse in 1453 CE, more than 2,200 years had come and gone. Rome as an idea, as an empire, had grown from a small village on a small hill in central Italy to dominate the known world, only to contract again, not in the original capital, but into a city nearly 1,000 miles away. As a political entity, the idea of Rome lasted an astonishingly long time.

To walk in the Forum, to amble the avenues and alleyways of Rome is to connect with a distant past that still speaks to us today. To admire, to wonder at the great antiquity and magnificent architecture of this once-great civilization is to remember the profound influence of the Romans, not just in their own world, but in ours as well. We are left to reflect on the greatness of what they built and the enormity of what they accomplished; we cannot help but be affected by the experience. After any time in the Eternal City, we are changed. No matter where we came from, no matter where we go, after spending time in the city we leave, ever after, all a little Roman ourselves. To go to Rome is to become a Roman.

Long after its power declined, Rome held a center place in the hearts and minds of untold millions. The prestige of Rome is immortal. The people who claimed sovereignty over it were not. In 610 CE, just two years after the column erected in his honor was completed, Phocas was overthrown and murdered in Constantinople. As the saying goes, live by the sword, die by the sword. His corpse was mutilated and burned. The statue atop the column was toppled and melted down. But the column and the pediment still stand just where they did more than 1,400 years ago. The Column of Phocas might have been the last monument constructed in the Forum, but it doesn't end the story of Rome. Rather, it merely signifies the end of a chapter. Rome's long, complex history is still being written.

➤ How to get to the Column of Phocas

The Column of Phocas is located on the Via Sacra, in the middle of the Roman Forum. It is an eight-minute walk from both the Colosseo Metro Station (Line B) and the Colosseum.

Address: Via Sacra, Roman Forum.

➤ Local eats

Start your day right at a great spot for breakfast or brunch:
Bar La Licata ($)
Via Dei Serpenti 165, Corner Via Leonina 1/A, 00184
+39 06 488 4746
http://barlalicata.it/

Satisfy your sweet tooth at a yummy bakery with a French influence:
Antico Forno ai Serpenti ($)
Via Dei Serpenti 122, 00184
+39 06 4542 7920
www.anticofornoaiserpenti.it/

Make your selection from a cocktail hour buffet with tapas, pastas, salads, and more:
Urbana 47 ($$)
Via Urbana 47, 00184
+39 335 705 8398
www.urbana47.it/en/

➤ Want a little more of the story before we wrap up? *Stop by the Basilica of San Clemente.*

If you are making your way between the Lateran and the Colosseum, you will likely pass an inconspicuous entrance to yet another church. With so many sights to see, there's nothing terribly noteworthy from the outside to capture your imagination, but step in and explore the Basilica of San Clemente. Despite the humble exterior, it has an extraordinary story to tell, one that outshines many of its more ornate cousins. Well, not one story, San Clemente tells several. In a way, no building more completely embodies the history of Rome.

When you enter the building, you are standing in a church built around 1100 CE. At the time it was built, Rome was a backwater, with a population just a fraction of what it had been centuries earlier. The church is a wonderful example of medieval architecture. But there's more.

Off to the side is the entrance to a museum. Pay and go downstairs. What lies at street level is only the beginning. The basilica is built on the foundations of a much older complex. It's when you start to descend that San Clemente begins to shine as the wonder it really is.

The first level down brings you to the rise of Christianity. There are the foundations of a 4th century CE basilica.

The exterior of the basilica. Photographs are not allowed inside, so it is difficult to show the different archaeological levels that make this one of the most fascinating buildings in all of Rome. The humble entrance does not hint at the extraordinary experience that awaits inside . . . and below.

This, in turn, was built from the home of a Roman nobleman, part of which had been used as a church as early as the 1st century CE. In an age of Christian persecution, having a church in your home took courage. Christian worship could lead to imprisonment and death. In this complex, we see the spread of Christianity, from a secret and illegal cult in the 1st century CE, to a legitimized religion in the 4th. This complex signifies the triumph of Christianity as the dominant force of Roman religious life.

If this was all there was, San Clemente would be extraordinary. But there is still more. The basement of the nobleman's house also contained a pagan shrine to the god Mithras. You can see the altar, and easily imagine the cult rituals. Separated by just a floor within the same building, the Mithraeum and the early church remind us all that the Christian world and the pagan one intermingled for centuries.

But there is more still. All of this was built on top of an even older structure, dating all the way back to the Republic. There are the foundations of a villa and a warehouse that were destroyed by the Great Fire in 64 CE. By descending to the lowest levels, you come face to face with an event so cataclysmic, it is still taught in schools today.

San Clemente is a gift. It is a cross-section of Roman history spanning more than a millennium, with connections to the Republic, the Emperors, the conflict between Christian and pagan, the domination of the Catholic Church, and so many points in between.

It also makes you wonder: If there are so many layers underneath this one minor church, then what is beneath all the buildings of the modern world? What untold treasures are yet to be discovered? With every footfall, consider: What lies beneath? What stories are waiting to be discovered?

Address: Via Labicana, 95.

Nearest Metro: Colosseo, Metro Line B. An eight-to-ten-minute walk from both the Metro and the Colosseum.

➤ Hours

Monday through Saturday from 9:00 a.m. to 12:30 p.m. and from 3:00 p.m. to 6:00 p.m.; Sundays and holidays from noon to 6:00 p.m.

Visit *www.basilicasanclemente.com* for up-to-date information.

BIBLIOGRAPHY

Appian. *The Civil Wars*. Translated by John M. Carter. London: Penguin Books, 1996.

Beard, Mary. *SPQR*. London: Profile Books, 2016.

Caesar, Julius, and Frederick Percy Long. *The Civil War*. New York: Barnes & Noble Books, 2005.

Cary, M. *A History of Rome*. London: Macmillan, 1954.

Cassius, Dio, Earnest Cary, and Herbert Baldwin Foster. *Roman History*. Cambridge, MA: Harvard University Press, 1927.

Champlin, Edward. *Nero*. Cambridge, MA: Belknap, 2005.

Dando-Collins, Stephen. *The Great Fire of Rome*. Cambridge, MA: Da Capo Press, 2010.

Everitt, Anthony. *Augustus*. New York: Random House, 2006.

———. *The Rise of Rome*. New York: Random House, 2012.

Gibbon, Edward, and H.R. Trevor-Roper. *The Decline and Fall of the Roman Empire*. New York: A.A. Knopf, 1993.

Grant, Michael. *The Roman Emperors*. New York: Barnes & Noble, 1997.

Goldsworthy, Adrian. *Augustus*. New Haven, CT: Yale University Press, 2014.

———. *Caesar*. New Haven, CT: Yale University Press, 2006.

Holland, Tom. *Dynasty*. Knopf Doubleday Publishing Group, 2015.

———. *Rubicon*. New York: Doubleday, 2003.

Jones, B.W. *The Emperor Domitian*. London: Routledge, 1992.

Laurén, Giles, and Francis W. Kelsey. *Caesar's Commentaries*. United States: Sophron Imprimit, 2012.

Magie, David. *Historia Augusta, Volume I*. Harvard University Press, 1921.

———. *Historia Augusta, Volume II*. Harvard University Press, 1924.

———. *Historia Augusta, Volume III*. Harvard University Press, 1932.

McLynn, Frank. *Marcus Aurelius*. Boston, MA: Da Capo Press, 2009.

Meier, Christian. *Caesar.* Translated by David McLintock. New York, NY: Basic Books, 1996.

Plutarch. *Greek and Roman Lives.* Translated by John Dryden and Arthur Hugh Clough. Mineola, NY: Dover Publications, 2005.

Potter, D.S. *Constantine the Emperor.* New York: Oxford University Press, 2013.

Sallust. *The Jugurthine War/The Conspiracy of Catiline.* Translated and with an introduction by S.A. Handford. Harmondsworth: Penguin, 1963.

Stambaugh, John E. *The Ancient Roman City.* Baltimore: Johns Hopkins University Press, 1992.

Strauss, Barry. *The Death of Caesar.* New York, NY: Simon & Schuster, 2015.

Suetonius. *The Twelve Caesars.* Translated by Robert Graves and J.B. Rives. London: Penguin Books, 2007.

Tacitus. *The Complete Works of Tacitus.* Translated by Alfred John Church, William Jackson Brodribb, and Moses Hadas. New York: Modern Library, 1942.

Walker, Charles. *Wonders of the Ancient World.* London: Popular Press, 1988.

Winterling, Aloys. *Caligula.* Berkeley: University of California Press, 2011.

ACKNOWLEDGMENTS

I am profoundly lucky to be surrounded and supported by countless amazing people. To say thank you to all would quadruple the length of the book. I want everyone to know that I am overwhelmed with gratitude.

I do need to mention a few people individually.

This humble book would not be possible without the love and support of my wife Erin, for whom no amount of "thank yous" will ever be sufficient.

My children, Ethan, Everett, and Harper for being the Best.Kids.Ever.

My mom, Kathy Barlag, for being a great travel companion and sounding board, who always keeps me grounded, and my father, Bruce, a great friend and mentor, who always reminds me to not get too grounded! I appreciate that you are always there.

My sisters Katie and Amy, who show me the love (and buy my books, even though they don't have to).

Pat and Sean, who are unconditional in their support and excitement.

My agent, John Willig, without whom this book would have never happened.

My dear friend Ryan Masters, who is always there with advice and encouragement.

My colleagues at World 50, for all they do every day. A special thanks to Salem Vance, and to Jeff Shulman, for his steadfast friendship.

The team at Career Press/New Page Books for their support, and going on this adventure together.

Everyone who has shown me support and shared my excitement, thank you. From the bottom of my heart, thank you.

INDEX

Index

Index

Index

Index

Index

ABOUT THE AUTHOR

Phillip Barlag is an executive director at World 50, which initiates and facilitates the most interesting and influential business conversations in the world. He is the author of *The Leadership Genius of Julius Caesar: Modern Lessons from the Man Who Built an Empire* (2016, Berrett-Kohler). He lives in the Atlanta, Georgia, area with his wife and three children.